BUILDING
HISTORY
SERIES

THE GREAT
WALL OF
CHINA

BUILDING
HISTORY
SERIES

THE GREAT

WALL OF

CHINA

by Tim McNeese

Lucent Books, Inc., San Diego, California

Library of Congress Cataloging-in-Publication Data

McNeese, Tim.
    The Great Wall of China / by Tim McNeese.
      p.   cm. — (Building history series)
    Includes bibliographical references and index.
    Summary: Historical examination of the building of China's
Great Wall.
    ISBN 1-56006-428-5 (alk. paper)
    1. Great Wall of China (China)—History—Juvenile literature.
[1. Great Wall of China (China)—History.]   I. Title. II. Series.
  DS793.G67M33   1997
  931—DC21   96-29937
                                                                   CIP
                                                                   AC
                                                                   RW

Printed in the U.S.A.

CONTENTS

FOREWORD

Throughout history, as civilizations have evolved and prospered, each has produced unique buildings and architectural styles. Combining the need for both utility and artistic expression, a society's buildings, particularly its large-scale public structures, often reflect the individual character traits that distinguish it from other societies. In a very real sense, then, buildings express a society's values and unique characteristics in tangible form. As scholar Anita Abromovitz comments in her book *People and Spaces*, "Our ways of living and thinking—our habits, needs, fear of enemies, aspirations, materialistic concerns, and religious beliefs—have influenced the kinds of spaces that we build and that later surround and include us."

That specific types and styles of structures constitute an outward expression of the spirit of an individual people or era can be seen in the diverse ways that various societies have built palaces, fortresses, tombs, churches, government buildings, sports arenas, public works, and other such monuments. The ancient Greeks, for instance, were a supremely rational people who originated Western philosophy and science, including the atomic theory and the realization that the earth is a sphere. Their public buildings, epitomized by Athens's magnificent Parthenon temple, were equally rational, emphasizing order, harmony, reason, and above all, restraint.

By contrast, the Romans, who conquered and absorbed the Greek lands, were a highly practical people preoccupied with acquiring and wielding power over others. The Romans greatly admired and readily copied elements of Greek architecture, but modified and adapted them to their own needs. "Roman genius was called into action by the enormous practical needs of a world empire," wrote historian Edith Hamilton. "Rome met them magnificently. Buildings tremendous, indomitable, amphitheaters where eighty thousand could watch a spectacle, baths where three thousand could bathe at the same time."

In medieval Europe, God heavily influenced and motivated the people, and religion permeated all aspects of society, molding people's worldviews and guiding their everyday actions. That spiritual mindset is reflected in the most important medieval structure—the Gothic cathedral—which, in a sense, was a model of heavenly cities. As scholar Anne Fremantle so elegantly phrases it, the cathedrals were "harmonious elevations of stone and glass reaching up to heaven to seek and receive the light [of God]."

Our more secular modern age, in contrast, is driven by the realities of a global economy, advanced technology, and mass communications. Responding to the needs of international trade and the growth of cities housing millions of people, today's builders construct engineering marvels, among them towering skyscrapers of steel and glass, mammoth marine canals, and huge and elaborate rapid transit systems, all of which would have left their ancestors, even the Romans, awestruck.

In examining some of humanity's greatest edifices, Lucent Books' Building History Series recognizes this close relationship between a society's historical character and its buildings. Each volume in the series begins with a historical sketch of the people who erected the edifice, exploring their major achievements as well as the beliefs, customs, and societal needs that dictated the variety, functions, and styles of their buildings. A detailed explanation of how the selected structure was conceived, designed, and built, to the extent that this information is known, makes up the majority of the volume.

Each volume in the Lucent Building History Series also includes several special features that are useful tools for additional research. A chronology of important dates gives students an overview, at a glance, of the evolution and use of the structure described. Sidebars create a broader context by adding further details on some of the architects, engineers, and construction tools, materials, and methods that made each structure a reality, as well as the social, political, and/or religious leaders and movements that inspired its creation. Useful maps help the reader locate the nations, cities, streets, and individual structures mentioned in the text; and numerous diagrams and pictures illustrate tools and devices that bring to life various stages of construction. Finally, each volume contains two bibliographies, one for student research, the other listing works the author consulted in compiling the book.

Taken as a whole, these volumes, covering diverse ancient and modern structures, constitute not only a valuable research tool, but also a tribute to the human spirit, a fascinating exploration of the dreams, skills, ingenuity, and dogged determination of the great peoples who shaped history.

IMPORTANT DATES IN THE BUILDING OF THE GREAT WALL OF CHINA

B.C.
4000
Asian people develop agriculture, which results in their settling in villages, often surrounded by protective earthen walls.

The Great Wall

221–210
Reign of China's first emperor, Qin Shih Huang Ti; massive, long stretches of the wall are built under General Meng Tian's command.

B.C. 4000	3000	2000	1000	500	A.D. 500	750

1500
The rise of the Shang dynasty, during which the earliest Chinese cities are built and fortified with protective walls.

A.D.
581–604
Sui emperor Wendi orders the construction of hundreds of miles of new Chinese border walls.

481–221
Warring States Period, during which China is a collection of hostile separate kingdoms bounded by protective walls known as the long ramparts.

186–40
Reign of the Han emperor Wu Di, who extends the Great Wall far into western territories of China to protect the lucrative trade along the Silk Road.

1644–1912
The Manchu hold China for nearly three centuries, during which the Great Wall ceases to serve as a grand defensive border between China and the northern barbarian tribes.

1446
During the reign of Zheng Tong, the Ming work out an elaborate signaling code for those garrisoned along the Great Wall.

1949
Communist revolutionaries led by Mao Zedong come to power.

1644
The Manchu dynasty rises to power; with the passing of the Ming dynasty, the glory days of the Great Wall of China come to an end.

1368
Rebellion by Han Chinese ends Mongol occupation of China.

1984
Deng Xiaoping, leader of the Communist Party in China, orders the restoration of the Great Wall.

| 1000 | 1250 | 1500 | 1750 | 1950 | 1975 | 2000 |

1368–1644
Reign of the Ming dynasty.

1960s
Mao Zedong decrees that anything ancient should be destroyed, including the Great Wall; as a result, hundreds of miles of the Wall are torn down.

1260
Kublai Khan becomes Mongol emperor and consolidates Mongolian control over China; the Great Wall remains a limited barrier to northern barbarian invasion.

1899
American newspaper reporters run false story about American engineers intending to tear down the Great Wall; ensuing panic in China leads to the Boxer Rebellion in the summer of 1900.

1572–1620
Ming emperor Wanli orders many changes in the Great Wall, rebuilding portions of the Wall and adding granite block towers.

ca. 1162–1227
Mongol invasion of China; Genghis Khan breaches the Great Wall; conquers Peking in 1215.

INTRODUCTION

Thousands of years ago, a people in Asia began to build something unlike anything else on earth. Called the Great Wall of China, it is the longest structure ever built. Like a sleeping dragon, the mysterious Wall snakes its way across the northern provinces of China, from the Pacific Coast at its eastern end to its western end in the Gobi Desert. Between its two endpoints, the Great Wall of China winds across frozen plains, rugged mountains, and dry, sandy plateaus.

Never, in ancient times or modern, has anyone built a monument that matches the form, scope, and dimension of the Great Wall. It is unique in design as well as length. The sheer volume of materials used in building the Wall is staggering. It has been estimated that the Great Wall contains enough stone, brick, and rubble to form a wall eight feet high and three feet thick encircling the equator, a distance of approximately twenty-five thousand miles. In his book *The Great Wall of China*, Robert Silverberg describes the engineering triumph that the Great Wall represents:

Like a stone serpent, the Great Wall of China slithers over the peaks and dips of the Chinese landscape. In addition to its beautiful architecture, the Great Wall has protected China from invaders throughout the country's history.

WHERE EXACTLY IS THE GREAT WALL?

In some ways the Great Wall remains a mystery, even to the Chinese people themselves. As far as can be determined, the Wall has never been surveyed in its entirety. No one has ever accurately placed its course on a map. Even modern maps typically show the Great Wall on a course plotted centuries ago by three Jesuit priests who were working for the Qing emperor Kangxi. The Priests' map, since lost, was given to the emperor in 1708. It is widely assumed that the Jesuits did not actually travel the entire length of the Great Wall. New maps are on the way, however. An aerial survey of the Wall has been ongoing since the early 1980s, but experts say that it will take decades to completely survey, catalog, and map it.

Not only is the Wall's exact course in question, but archaeologists have yet to adequately explore its complete length. Sections of the Wall that have survived intact over the centuries have been thoroughly studied, but there are still hundreds of miles of the Great Wall that remain untouched by modern surveyors, scientists, and geographers.

The Wall is an overwhelming thing. It is one of the wonders of the world, though not one of the ancient Seven Wonders of the World. That canon was drawn up by a Greek who knew of China, if at all, only as a legendary land somewhere in the cloud-shrouded east. Moreover, the last of the classical Seven Wonders was built in 280 B.C., six decades before [Emperor] Ch'in Shih Huang Ti (Qin Shi huangdi) embarked on his wall-building project. Of the original Seven Wonders, only the Pyramid of Khufu survives today. The Wall endures.

THE WALL'S TWISTING COURSE

The sheer size of the Great Wall is difficult to imagine. Various comparisons have been made to help people grasp the enormity of such an undertaking for the ancient Chinese. For example, if the Great Wall could be removed to Europe, it would surround all or most of France, Switzerland, Italy,

Austria, Hungary, Bulgaria, Romania, Poland, Russia, and the former Czechoslovakia and Yugoslavia. An English surveyor observing the Great Wall in 1793 estimated that just to build the Great Wall's watchtowers would require more stone and brick than had been used to build all the buildings in the London of his day.

Estimates of the Great Wall's length vary, in large part because throughout Chinese history several walls have been constructed. The Wall known today is not the result of a single project. The primary wall lying between Shanhaiguan in the east and Jiayuguan in the west measures 1,850 miles. This stretch of Wall, built between 1403 and 1424 during the Ming

CHINA'S PROVINCES

THE WALL AND ITS GEOGRAPHY

The Great Wall extends across three drastically different geographic regions. The western end of the Wall is anchored in desert lands, including the Gobi, a desert of half a million square miles in east-central Asia. Here the Wall is mostly in ruin and little of its original course can be found today.

The central sections of the Great Wall pass through what is often called the Mud Region. This area lies across the Ordos Steppes, where the great Chinese waterway, the Yellow River, follows a winding course, first running north, then east, and then south, forming something close to a gigantic horseshoe. The Ordos consists of forty thousand square miles of yellowish, sandy soil and quicksand. Historically, it was here that Genghis Khan, the fearsome leader of the Mongols to the north, breached the Great Wall in the thirteenth century A.D. Even today, local village people say that as the wind whistles at night across the sandy dunes of the Ordos, they can still hear the fighting between ancient Chinese soldiers and Mongolian invaders. Legend also has it that a horse belonging to the first true Chinese emperor, Qin Shih Huang Ti, laid out the route of the ancient wall across the Ordos. As the story goes, a saddle was fastened to the horse's tail and dragged along the ground as the animal walked, marking the route of the Great Wall.

East of the Ordos region, the Great Wall stretches across the precipitous mountains of eastern China. For part of the route, the Wall follows the Yellow River. As the great stone dragon approaches the ancient city of Peking (modern Beijing) it loops 250 miles north around the city. This section is in better shape than any other portion of the Wall. Once past Beijing, the Wall winds its way over a high mountain range to the Yellow Sea. Its final miles end in a coastal fortress, called a citadel, located on the Gulf of Liaotung. The Wall even continues out into the gulf to form a jetty, a structure designed to protect the harbor. Tradition says that the jetty was built "on vast ships which were sunk voluntarily to provide foundations."

Visitors walk through a restored section of the Wall. Even today, the Great Wall remains an enduring symbol of China's rich history.

dynasty, made use of earlier walls. However, if all the Great Wall's extensions and supplementary routes are included, its total length approaches 4,000 miles. Jonathan Fryer, in his book *The Great Wall of China*, explains the difficulty in determining the exact length of the Wall, noting, "Nobody has ever seen the whole length of the Wall, and no two authoritative maps agree as to its exact course."

Frequently, the Great Wall, with its meandering course, which hugs the curves and dips of many mountain chains, is compared to a dragon. At Shanhaiguan Pass, where the Wall begins in the east, stand guard towers that have been referred to for centuries as the Old Dragon's Head. The Wall then represents the great dragon's twisting body. The symbolism is important to the Chinese: Traditionally, the dragon has been a revered Asian symbol of strength and energy.

AN ENGINEERING FEAT

Certainly, constructing this immense barrier required strength and energy. All of its thousands of miles were erected centuries ago without the aid of sophisticated equipment or a nonmanual power source. The work was done by hundreds of thousands of human beings and draft animals. Sections of the Great Wall near Beijing, for example, consist of two-ton granite stones erected to a height of twenty feet. Atop this base, the ancient workers built stone parapets, or low walls along its edges, for protection, rising an additional five feet. Between the parapets, the Wall features a paved road wide enough to accommodate five mounted horses galloping side by side. This basic wall design required the fine cutting of thousands of granite stones for each mile of construction, and all of the work was done by hand. Moreover, such labor-intensive endeavor was complicated by the twisting and turning mountains of China's highlands. In some places the Wall climbs over peaks nearly two miles in height.

The modern Chinese writer Luo Zewen, who has visited the Great Wall, gives his perspective on the engineering feat that the Wall represents:

> Standing on Juyongguan, Badaling, Shanhaiguan, or Jiayuguan pass, one cannot help marveling at the Great Wall seen winding like a snake among the towering mountains. Since we today are invariably out of breath from climbing the wall empty-handed, it must have been strenuous indeed for the builders in ancient times to carry the bricks weighing more than ten kilograms apiece (or 22 pounds), and stone slabs weighing hundreds of kilograms, to the mountain tops and ridges. They paid dearly in sweat and blood for this project. The building, and continual rebuilding, of this structure is of course a technical subject—but when we consider the technical means available at the time of its construction, we realize that this is a human story after all, a testimony to human will and perseverance.

THE BEGINNINGS OF A WALL-BUILDING TRADITION

The Chinese were building walls long before construction of the Great Wall of China was begun. Around 4000 B.C., the people of ancient China, till then nomadic hunters of wild game, developed agriculture. Tending to crops and fields kept them in one place; temporary farming settlements and then permanent villages began to spring up. It was in such ancient villages that the first Chinese walls were built, to guard against attacks by neighboring villagers.

Several such Neolithic, or New Stone Age, walls have been unearthed. Some of the best preserved sites are located in the

The ancient Chinese began raising crops around 4000 B.C. Unlike nomadic hunters, farmers tended to remain in one place, and agricultural communities became the first permanent villages.

16

Using the hang-t'u *method, Chinese workers fill a wooden frame—a mold for a wall—with earth. Two other workers, standing within the framework, use pounding instruments to tightly pack the earth and minimize settling. This process is repeated until the frame is full. When the frame is removed, a wall of tightly packed earth remains.*

Shensi province, where archaeologists uncovered remnants of a protective perimeter wall that once surrounded a village. The wall measures about 400 by 450 yards, stood nearly 20 feet high, and was about 27 feet wide across its top. Such walls were erected by a primitive but efficient method of wall construction known as the *hang-t'u* method.

The name comes from two Chinese words, *hang*, meaning pounded or beaten, and *t'u*, which translates as "earth." Builders began by constructing a frame of wood planks or bamboo. This formed the mold for the wall. Earth was then unloaded into the mold and packed tightly to minimize settling with prolonged use. The wall was slowly built up in layers, each perhaps only a few inches thick. Workers stood inside the framework and, using some type of ramming or pounding tool, beat the dirt down until firm. Peter Nancarrow, in his book *Early China and the Wall*, describes evidence of this packing technique in the unearthed wall remnants:

Chinese history is fraught with periods of intense warfare, as this battle illustration from A.D. 150 suggests. The earliest Chinese walls were probably created to serve as instruments of defense.

The first noticeable thing about the wall is that it is made up of sharply defined layers of earth, each about five inches (thirteen centimeters) thick. Secondly, the top surface of the uppermost layer can be seen to be covered all over with shallow dents, all roughly the same shape, as if they were all made by the same object.

When a layer of earth was adequately compacted, more dirt was thrown into the mold, and the process was repeated. Once the wall reached the desired height, the workers pulled the forms off the wall, leaving a stable and extremely durable mass of tightly packed earth.

A CULTURE AT THE CENTER OF THE WORLD

China's wall-building tradition probably grew out of a specific need. Wars against outside invaders and skirmishes between neighboring Chinese kingdoms are a constant in Chinese history. The walls were no doubt intended to protect territory and repel invaders set on conquest. However, this defense tactic sometimes succeeded and sometimes failed, leading historians to suggest that China's walls may have had more symbolic than practical value.

The ancient Chinese thought of their country as both the geographical center of the world and the only cultured civilization in it. This belief was not altogether unfounded. The Chinese possessed a written language as long ago as 1500 B.C. and were the first people to develop the compass, paper, porcelain, and silk cloth. The ancient Chinese developed a powerful and efficient system of government, built great cities, and created magnificent works of literature and art. Over the centuries, other Asian cultures demonstrated their high esteem for Chinese civilization by borrowing elements of China's art, language, literature, religion, and technology.

MAINTAINING SUPERIORITY

China's view of itself within the ancient world may have contributed to its wall-building tradition. Believing themselves superior to their non-Chinese neighbors, the Chinese resisted outside influences. They also sought to prevent the spread of Chinese culture to neighbors they considered inferior and unworthy of the fruits of Chinese civilization. In an effort to remain separate from other peoples, historians suggest, China surrounded itself with walls. Writer Robert Silverberg explains:

A well-preserved segment of embroidered silk from about the third century is but one example of China's rich culture.

The Wall has long been a symbol of the Chinese way of doing things. When the Romans were troubled by barbarians on their borders, they marched into the outlands and conquered their enemy. The Chinese built a Wall. They withdrew behind a barrier which, for all its awesome breadth, is as much a monument to futility as to anything else. The Wall had psychological value to the Chinese more than it had real military worth. It is the brick-and-stone realization of an idea, a summing up of China's concept of the relationship between itself and the hostile outer world.

Put simply, anyone who was not Chinese was considered an outsider and a barbarian. Differences in language and lifestyle simply intensified the Chinese outlook, especially where China's northern neighbors were concerned. The languages of the northerners bore no resemblance to Chinese, and the northern peoples still lived as nomads, moving from place to place with their herds of goats and yaks. The Chinese no longer practiced a nomadic way of life. They were farmers; many Chinese remained on the same piece of land all their lives.

THREATS FROM WITHOUT

China's disdain for and mistrust of outsiders was not solely an outgrowth of its worldview. The fear of foreign invasion was real, especially in the north, where warriors of numerous nomadic tribes repeatedly raided Chinese border villages. Mounted on horseback, dressed in animal skins, the raiders stormed across the borders of the regional states of China to rob Chinese towns of their precious grain. Often, they terror-

The Chinese developed a written language as early as 1500 B.C. This and other achievements fueled China's belief that it was the most cultured civilization in the ancient world.

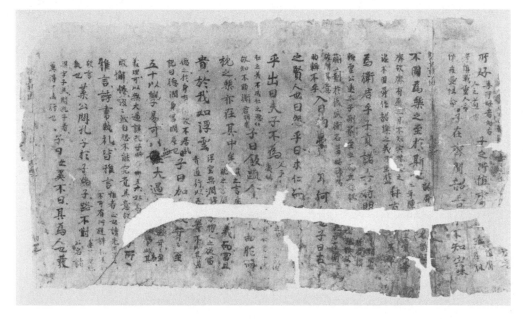

ized, killed, raped, and burned on their way. The Chinese could rightly refer to these invasions by the northern nomads as "barbaric." One witness, an English monk who worked as a missionary in China, described the violence:

> The detestable people of Satan . . . brake forth from their mountain-compassed and rock-defended region, like devils loosed out of Hell . . . like grasshoppers covering the face of the earth, spoiling the eastern confines with fire and sword, ruining cities, cutting up woods, rooting up vineyards, killing the people both of city and country. . . . They are rather monsters than men, thirsting and drinking blood, tearing and devouring the flesh of dogs and men; clothed with ox-hides, armed with iron plates; in stature thick and short, well set, strong in body; in war invincible.

In battle, the northern nomads had the advantage. Though few in number, they had greater mobility and speed because they rode horses and superiority in weapons because they had bows and arrows. These raiding armies moved quickly from one province to another before the Chinese could muster a response. Often, they awaited the start of the annual harvest of their southern neighbors before invading. Then they swept into farming villages and towns, seizing the newly cut wheat. Often, they took with them anything else they could carry, plundering the helpless village inhabitants.

Prior to the rise of the Qin dynasty in the third century B.C., northern nomads periodically invaded and conquered numerous Chinese provinces. As conquerors, the "barbarians" forced the Chinese to farm for them, keeping them as peasant workers.

Such invasions from the various tribes of nomadic northern Asians continued to plague the Chinese for hundreds of years. Writing in the late eighth century B.C., a Zhou dynasty poet describes the terror brought to his people by the Xianyun, a nomadic tribe:

> We have no house, no home
> Because of the Xianyun.
> We cannot rest or bide
> Because of the Xianyun.
> Yes, we must be always on our guard;
> The Xianyun are very swift.

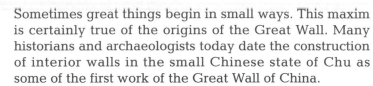

THE GREAT WALL OF CHU

Sometimes great things begin in small ways. This maxim is certainly true of the origins of the Great Wall. Many historians and archaeologists today date the construction of interior walls in the small Chinese state of Chu as some of the first work of the Great Wall of China.

In 656 B.C., a Chu prince named Zheng Wang ordered construction of a long wall called Fang Zheng. This wall, intended to keep out invaders from the neighboring Chinese state of Qi, to the east, stretched for approximately three hundred miles. Shaped like a semicircle, the wall ran from a northwestern county in the modern Hubei Province in a northerly direction through Shaanxi and Henan Provinces and ended in Miyang County.

Though much of this construction was of the *hang-t'u* method of pounding earth into a wood or bamboo mold, some portions of this early wall were built of stone. Modern archaeologists have discovered stone remnants in the Shaanxi Province extending for over sixty miles. At some points along its course, ancient portals and gates are still visible.

The Chu walls are considered important in China's history of wall building. They set the design and pattern for later generations and dynasties of wall builders, and these early walls occasionally served their military purpose, as in 624 when invaders from the neighboring state of Jin attacked the Chu. Their invasion was halted by this early model of a Chinese defensive barrier.

THREATS FROM WITHIN

Clashes between neighboring Chinese states were often just as destructive. China's history is fraught with territorial disputes between kingdoms. The period from 481 through 221 B.C., for example, was so violent it became known as the Warring States Period, 260 years of constant fighting. At this time, China was a cluster of states headed by a hereditary monarch who gradually lost control to powerful nobles ruling small kingdoms, seven of which—Qi, Chu, Qin, Zhao, Han, Yan, and Wei—emerged as dominant.

During these years, walls went up all across China to protect one state from the next and to define the territories each ruler claimed. Called long ramparts, the walls surrounded entire states. The building of the long ramparts required tens of thousands of laborers, months of planning, and careful organization. The walls themselves consisted of layers of tamped earth and baked clay bricks. Some walls also contained reeds

A figure of a warrior, reminiscent of those who fought during the Warring States Period.

for added strength. Historian Robert Silverberg describes the efforts that went into the building of the long ramparts:

> To build these walls, which were hundreds of miles long, vast aggregations of laborers had to be assembled. The fact that they were built at all testifies to the strength of the feudal lord in each of the wall-building states. . . . The Dukes of Qin, Jin, Qi, and other individual states were able to command the necessary labor forces, though even they could not yet mobilize enough manpower to wall off every border. They had to be content with protecting those frontiers in greatest peril.

Within a span of about 150 years, from approximately 450 to 300 B.C., the states of Qi, Wei, Yan, Zhao, and Qin built hun-

THE GREAT WALL OF YAN

One of the longest walls constructed during the Warring States Period was a barrier erected in the northern state of Yan. In ancient China, Yan was a large province located in northeastern China, hugging the Bo Hai, an interior arm of the Yellow Sea. Modern-day Beijing is located in this ancient Chinese state.

The leaders of Yan built walls along its northern and southern borders: The northern wall was intended to keep out the Donghu people of Inner Mongolia, while the southern walls were meant to block invasions from southern Chinese neighbors. The southern wall was called the Great Wall of Yishui, as its course followed that of the Yishui River. This series of walls was constructed in the fourth century B.C. and extended to a length of approximately 150 miles.

The northern Yan wall was much longer than its southern counterpart. One of the last walls built by any Chinese province prior to the founding of the Qin dynasty in 221 B.C., this eight-hundred-mile wall was the longest constructed by the ancient Chinese. Remnants can still be seen today in the modern Chinese provinces of Hebei and Liaoning, ending in the east in the city of Liaoyang.

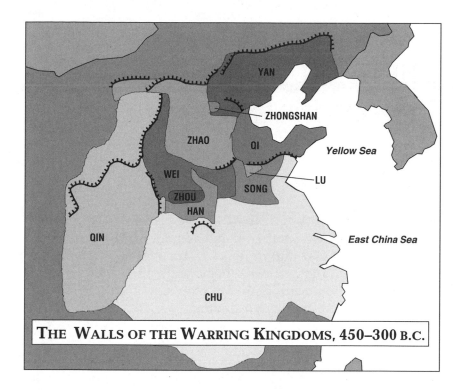

YAN

ZHONGSHAN

ZHAO

QI

Yellow Sea

WEI

LU

ZHOU

SONG

HAN

QIN

East China Sea

CHU

THE WALLS OF THE WARRING KINGDOMS, 450–300 B.C.

dreds of miles of walls, essentially serving notice that the territory within the walls was not up for grabs. This deterrent was not always successful, however.

One ancient writing describes the military campaign of one Chinese king, Wu Ling of Zhao, as he worked his way toward nearby Qin: "[Wu Ling] set out . . . at the head of his war councilors, to the northwest, and won possession of the Hu territory in that region, with the intention of making an attack southward . . . to invade Qin [the Chinese province to the west]."

These early walls have no direct connection to the Great Wall of China. Rather, their significance lies in the fact that they mark the beginnings of the Chinese wall-building tradition, strengthened over hundreds of years.

THE WALL OF
TEN THOUSAND *LI*

By the fourth century B.C., the Chinese provinces had formed alliances against one another in an extended struggle for dominance. Through war and diplomacy, the states of Chu in the south and Qin in the northwest became dominant. In time, this development would dramatically alter the course of China's history and its wall-building tradition.

For a few decades, the two states existed in relative balance, each ruling its own sphere of influence. However, over time Qin rose to dominance. Beginning in 312 B.C., Qin, whose alternative spelling, Ch'in, is the source of the name China, waged a relentless campaign to gain control of all China. The extremely capable Qin military not only kept northern barbarians out of the province, but enabled the Qin dynasty to expand in China at the expense of its Chinese neighbors. This extensive military campaign of dominance began its final stage in 246 B.C.

In that year a fourteen-year-old boy named Zheng (often written as Cheng) came to power in the state of Qin. Through military might, cruelty, and bloodshed, Zheng toppled rulers in provinces across China, uniting the country under his rule before reaching his fortieth birthday. In 221 B.C., Zheng adopted a new title for himself, Qin Shih Huang Ti, or First Sovereign Emperor of the Qin. His subjects typically referred to him as the Only First. As China's first emperor, Zheng oversaw the construction of much of what has come to be known as the Great Wall of China.

THE EMPEROR QIN SHIH HUANG TI

Sima Qian, a famous Chinese historian, wrote this description of Qin Shih Huang Ti nearly a century after the emperor's death:

The king of Qin is a man with a prominent nose, large eyes, a chest like a bird of prey; with the voice of a jackal; a man of little kindness; a heart of a tiger, or that of a wolf. . . . He finds it easy to act humble toward people: as soon as he obtains what he wants, he finds it just as easy to devour them.

Qin's rule over a unified China was brief, only eleven years. However, his legacy is important. Once Qin had eliminated most internal opposition and united the various provinces, he saw no need for the internal walls that previously divided them.

Qin Shih Huang Ti, China's first emperor. After Qin welded the various Chinese provinces into one nation, he commenced construction on the Great Wall.

ETERNAL SOLDIERS GUARD EMPEROR'S TOMB

The first of China's Great Wall builders, Qin Shih Huang Ti's story is one of mystery and treachery. His origins were humble. At birth he was named Zheng, the son of a concubine of a merchant named Lu Buwei. Lu gave the girl to a Qin prince named Zichu, who was unaware that she was already pregnant by Lu. When Zheng was born, he was accepted as the son of the prince. In 250 B.C., Zichu became king of Qin. Upon his death four years later, Zheng, fourteen-year-old son of a merchant, became ruler. Once he reached manhood in 235, Zheng began expanding his power outside the province of Qin.

Despite his simple origins, Qin's rule was one of great wealth. Once in power, he promoted costly building projects within his kingdom. One of those architectural wonders was revealed in the spring of 1974. Chinese peasants in the Yen Tsai commune in Lin-t'ung made a tremendous archaeological discovery: a vast underground collection of life-size pottery statues of soldiers and horses, complete with chariots, all created to guard the now twenty-two-hundred-year-old tomb of Qin Shih Huang Ti. The figures were buried in a gigantic three-acre vault, covered over with a dirt and wooden framework.

The figures in the vault cover an area measuring seven hundred feet by two hundred feet. Archaeologists claim that the soldiers are arranged just as a live honor guard would have been lined up for battle under Emperor Qin. The arms, legs, and torso of each is much the same as the next, but the face of every figure is unique. Each face is covered with a thick layer of plaster and was probably modeled after an actual living soldier in Qin's guard.

A ghostly relic of the pottery army entombed to guard the grave of Qin. Its face was probably modeled after an actual soldier in Qin's guard.

Sometime in the past, the vault roof collapsed, and many of the statues have broken limbs or are smashed completely. But soldier figures have been removed relatively intact. In addition, other items have been discovered in the vault, including "gold, jade, bamboo, and bone artifacts, as well as linen, silk, pottery utensils, bronze objects, and iron farm tools." Archaeologists have also unearthed metal swords and arrowheads, many of which were treated during Qin's rule with a preservative that has kept the weapons of war from rusting or corroding.

Modern archaeologists speculate as to Qin having thousands of statues made for his tomb's protection. In fact, for all his recorded cruelty, Qin's use of terra cotta soldiers and horses perhaps should be seen as a humane act on his part. Earlier Chinese dynasties, such as the Shang (1700–1100 B.C.), buried live soldiers with their deceased emperors. By using pottery statues, Qin continued the ancient practice only symbolically.

Although the vault of pottery guards has been uncovered, archaeologists continue to search for the actual tomb of Qin Shih Huang Ti. The tomb is described in ancient texts as extraordinarily elaborate, constructed in Qin's extravagant style. According to Chinese historian Sima Qian:

According to archaeologists, the life-size figures are arranged in real battle formation.

> As soon as the First Emperor became king of Qin, excavations and building had been started at Mount Li, while after he won the empire, more than 700,000 conscripts from all parts of the country worked there. They dug through three subterranean streams and poured molten copper for the outer coffin, and the tomb was filled with models of palaces, pavilions and offices, as well as fine vessels, precious stones, and rarities. Artisans were ordered to fix up crossbows so that any thief breaking in would be shot. All the country's streams, the Yellow River, and the Yangtze were reproduced in quicksilver [mercury] and by some mechanical means made to flow into a miniature ocean.

How much of this tomb is intact today remains a mystery. While the search for Qin's tomb continues, archaeologists do not expect to find the tomb as it was left originally. According to Sima Qian, Qin's tomb, which was sealed shut in 210 B.C., was broken into by robbers and desecrated just four years after the great emperor's death.

So these walls were systematically destroyed, as a stone tablet unearthed at Qinhuangdao testifies. Erected after an inspection tour by Qin of former eastern wall fortifications, the marker reads:

> After I overpowered all the princes, China for the first time enjoyed peace. I have taken down all the old walls and passes and leveled the steep landscapes. Now the common people are pacified and no longer have any fear of war. Men work on the land, while women are likewise engaged in their work.

The destruction of China's internal walls notwithstanding, the potential for invasion from the outside still existed. Sima Qian wrote of the emperor's efforts to defend against the external threat. Qin conceived a vast wall measuring, according to Sima Qian, ten thousand *li*. Sima Qian's reference to the Wall's length is figurative. Although an inexact measurement, a traditional *li* was approximately one-third of a mile; thus, a ten-thousand-*li* wall would stretch over thirty-three hundred miles. However, the Wall referred to in the following passage measured about fifteen hundred miles:

> When Qin had unified the empire, Meng Tian was sent at the head of 300,000 men to put down the Rong (Jung) and Di (Ti) barbarians in the north. He seized the area south of the Yellow River and built a large wall which followed the terrain and made use of natural obstacles and passes. From Lintao in the west, it went all the way to the east of the Liao River—more than 10,000 *li*.

QIN'S NORTHERN BORDER BARRIER

It is during Qin's reign that the story of the Great Wall of China begins in earnest. Once Qin Shih Huang Ti had consolidated his power over greater China, an achievement symbolized by the destruction of China's internal walls, construction on the Great Wall commenced. Such a northern border wall was consistent with China's tradition of wall building to keep out barbarian invaders. But Qin's foreign policy was slightly more complicated than merely relying on the construction of a defensive wall.

First, he determined just where he wanted to fix his northern border. The northern border wall of the Qin state to the

A well-preserved section of the Wall shows its twisting, meandering course. While only fragments of Qin's Wall remain, the first emperor painstakingly began what would become the Great Wall of China.

west was still intact and would have been serviceable as a border, but Qin aimed for further expansion. A nomadic tribe known as the Xiongnu had settled north of the wall in the Ordos region. Qin soon launched a campaign to drive the Xiongnu farther north and enclose his newly seized territory with a new wall along the course of the Yellow River.

Qin intended his wall to serve as a cultural as well as physical barrier, designed to keep the "civilized" Chinese from having contact with the barbarians. His wall was to divide the rich, fertile farmland of the south from the arid northern steppe, treeless lands where the nomads grazed their flocks. However, separating the two regions was not a simple process. There was no clear division; the lands of the north shifted from fertile to barren gradually and irregularly. As a result, the Wall of Qin Shih Huang Ti ran through both regions rather than dividing them as Qin had wanted.

This created a problem for Qin. Farmers living in the territories south of his wall were sometimes attracted by fertile farmland on the other side. Once established north of the Wall, some transplanted farmers abandoned their farms and took up the nomadic way of life. Such a change might be prompted by

THE LEGEND OF MENG JIANGNU

The building of Qin Shih Huang Ti's Great Wall has inspired many stories and legends. Several versions of one such legend relate the story of Meng Jiangnu, daughter of a conscripted Wall worker. The Ballad of Meng begins with the marriage of the beautiful Meng to the handsome and scholarly Fan San-lang. Within weeks of their marriage, Fan San-lang was ordered to duty on the Great Wall.

Sorrowfully, Fan San-lang left Meng to join the workers on the Wall. Months passed and Meng heard nothing from her husband. As winter approached, she began sewing heavy clothing for him. Then one night Meng dreamed of her husband, who spoke these words to her:

> I am freezing to death he seemed to say.
> Quickly make for me a padded gown.
> Separated am I so far from the family,
> The wicked king has sent me to build the Great Wall
> Since boyhood by my books I bided. I have little
>   brute strength;
> How can I be expected to do this cruel work?

Then Fan San-lang told his beautiful bride that he was, in fact, already dead, having fallen from exhaustion, and that he was now buried inside the Wall itself. Upon awakening, Meng determined to travel to the Wall to see for herself if the dream was true. Arriving at the Wall, she began questioning workers for the whereabouts of her husband. They told her that her husband had indeed died and was buried in the Wall. Grief stricken, Meng Jiangnu began to weep. Her crying reached the ears of the spirit known as the Jade Emperor, who took pity on her and, with a clap of thunder, tore a gash "several *li* long" in the newly constructed Wall. The bones of thousands of peasant workers tumbled out from the Wall.

She removed her husband's bones from the others and began the long walk home to see to their burial.

Here, the story takes a decided twist, bringing the Emperor Qin directly into the plot line:

> Now hardly was she started on her long journey
> Than the wicked Qin Shih Huang Ti came by that way
> With officials and soldiers noble and numberless,

With spears, pikes and swords, like a forest of hemp.

Spying the beautiful Meng Jiangnu, the emperor invited her to come to his court as one of his concubines. If she refused, he told her, he would order her execution. Meng begged Qin to give her a hundred days to give him an answer. Qin agreed, but he ordered her to come to his court and sew him an embroidered cloak. "After that," he said, "I will allow you to go to your home and bury your husband's bones."

When the hundred days passed, Meng Jiangnu presented Qin with a beautiful gold and purple robe. Qin then went back on his word, unwilling to let this talented and lovely woman out of his grasp, refusing to let her leave to bury Fan San-lang and ordering her to become a member of his harem. Desperate, Meng agreed, pleading with the emperor to give her husband a formal funeral on a hillside looking over the Eastern Sea. Qin agreed.

Qin Shi Huang Ti ordered a grand funeral for Fan San-lang. His entire court was present and the emperor himself participated in the funeral ceremony. However, Qin was not to have his way. Once the services were completed and the bones of her husband were properly interred, Meng Jiangnu ran to the cliff's edge and jumped into the waters below, committing suicide before she would submit to the evil Qin, the one she held responsible for the death of her bright, young, frail husband.

The end of the story includes the words of the emperor, stunned at the act of desperation:

> To live alone for love is rare in the world;
> There are very few girls like this now to be found.
> Let a monument of stone be erected on this coast
> In memory of Meng Jiangnu, who jumped into the sea;
> And now make ready my chariot royal,
> For I will soon return into my Court.

Thus, Meng Jiangnu passes into popular legend, both she and her husband becoming symbolic martyrs in the construction of the Great Wall. Such stories speak to the hardship which befell workers on the Great Wall. They also reveal the popular opinion held by many Chinese that Qin's rule was one of extreme oppression and cruelty.

constant contact with northerners through trade, poor harvests, or occasional intermarriage between Chinese farming families and northern nomadics. In any case, Qin's barrier failed to halt northward migration.

Qin's idea of fostering amicable relations with several tribes just north of the Wall also backfired. He wanted to create a buffer zone of friendly northern tribes that would insulate his empire from the more northern tribes that held the Chinese in contempt. Qin came to rely on his empire's closest neighbors as a first defense against nomadic tribes who crossed the border to raid his villages.

At the same time, however, this strategy undermined his effort to prevent contact between his people and the people of the north. Several of the neighboring tribes north of the Wall abandoned their pastoral lifestyles and began to practice farming. In doing so, they became more like their southern neighbors and contact between the peoples living on both sides of the Wall increased. Historian Silverberg describes what happened next:

> As [the tribes near the Wall] grew more settled, they developed a keener interest in possessing the luxuries of the Chinese on the other side of the Wall. It became a regular occurrence for the people of the reservoir zones to penetrate the Wall and make themselves masters of northern China, and on several occasions masters of all China. The "friendly" barbarians, not the wilder nomads of the distant north, became the greatest threats to Chinese security.

Eager to begin construction, the emperor turned to a trusted and efficient military leader to organize the immense construction project. General Meng Tian (sometimes written as Meng T'ien) came from an important Chinese family whose members had served provincial rulers before Qin. His father, Meng Wu, had served as an adjutant general to Qin and had conquered the province of Chu in 223 B.C. Meng Tian himself had succeeded in bringing the province of Qi into the empire in 221.

AN EXTRAORDINARY FEAT

Meng Tian proved to be invaluable to Qin's wall-building program. Nearly all of the few surviving written sources describing Meng and his work credit him with completing a monumental task with extraordinary speed. Silverberg echoes ancient praise:

> Khufu, when he built his Great Pyramid at Giza, kept thousands of men busy for twenty years, and raised a great pile of stone. . . . Meng T'ien spent no more than seven years building the Great Wall, completing it about 214 B.C., and he had the advantage of being able to incorporate long sections of earlier walls into it. Nevertheless his accomplishment is more remarkable than that of the pyramid builder, for Meng T'ien worked in extremes of climate, under uncertain conditions in a newly pacified empire, with unruly barbarians roaming not far to the north. The Chinese general flung up his mighty rampart in broiling heat and in winter snow; he ascended mountains and pressed on through endless plains. Freezing gales, sizzling sandstorms, raging storms assailed the builders. On and on went the making of bricks, the digging of trenches, the pounding of clay.

The Wall stretched from Shanhaiguan, to the east, on the Yellow Sea to the desert mountains of the Ala country at Jiayuguan, a total distance of approximately 1,850 miles. This span constitutes approximately half the Wall's total length when branches and windings are included.

"THE LONGEST CEMETERY ON EARTH"

The toll on those who labored on the Wall was extraordinarily severe. The physical demands were extreme and living conditions were harsh. Writer Ronald Schiller describes the trials faced by workers:

> None of Qin's undertakings caused more suffering or cost more lives than the Great Wall. Nearly a million laborers were conscripted, many of them the intellectual elite of China. Housed in vermin-infested camps, working naked in summer, clad in skins and rags in winter, they died by the tens of thousands from exposure, disease, exhaustion and hunger. Their bodies, buried in the foundations together with those who were bricked up alive for failing to

THE ENDS OF THE WALL: SHANHAIGUAN AND JIAYUGUAN

Lengthy portions of Qin's wall, over the centuries, have so disintegrated that they are difficult to locate even by modern archaeologists. Yet, even today, monuments marking both ends of the original Wall survive, located at Shanhaiguan in the east and Jiayuguan in the desert lands of the west.

The city of Shanhaiguan today lies three miles from the ocean. The name Shanhaiguan is translated as Mount-Sea Barrier or Between Mountain and Sea. That the Great Wall of Qin ends abruptly at the shoreline indicates that the ruler did not fear invasion from the sea. The Wall seems to rise straight out of the sea, its granite stones all tumbling down at the water's edge, after centuries of beating by ferocious waves and endless wind. As the Wall enters the city of Shanhaiguan, it passes through a symbolic market point, a gate called Xiaotiandiyimen, which means Under Heaven, Number One Gate, or The First Gate in the World.

Far beyond the Shanhaiguan, the Wall continues its serpentine course across mountain and valley, lowlands and desert until it arrives in Jiayuguan, meaning Barrier of the Pleasant Valley. Here a monument stands bearing the inscription "The Martial Barrier of All under Heaven." This marks, technically, the end of the line for the Great Wall. Jiayuguan serves as the final city on the barrier's route and is often called the Jade Gate.

work hard enough, have earned the Wall the grim appellation of "the longest cemetery on earth."

Mistreatment and tyranny were the rule toward those who worked on the Great Wall. Convict laborers were treated most brutally; their heads were shaved and their faces blackened to identify them and an iron collar was clamped around their necks. And the abuse was not unique to men. One ancient Chinese historian wrote: "Ditches along the roadside were filled with corpses of men who had been forced into construction of the Great Wall and when men could no longer

The Qin Wall actually continues for a few miles beyond Jiayuguan, out into the desert lands, a region the Chinese call Kouwai, translated as Outside the Passes. Through this valley, camel caravans passed for hundreds of years between the eerie and bleak Gobi Desert and the distant yet visible mountains of Tibet. During the Han dynasty, the Wall was extended into this sandy wilderness, where, according to superstitious villagers and nomads, many demons lived. Historically, this region abounded with highwaymen who lurked behind rocks, ready to pounce on unsuspecting trade caravans. At Jiayuguan, another tablet bearing an inscription is found, one of fairly recent origin, which speaks of the nature of the place beyond the Jade Gate, beyond the Barrier of the Pleasant Valley, where thieves abound:

The Great Wall seems to rise from the ocean at Shanhaiguan, where it begins its serpentine course toward Jiayuguan.

> Looking West we see the vast road leading to the New Dominion
>
> But only brave ones go through the martial Barrier.

be found, their widows joined the march." Such practices explain why Qin was one of the most hated emperors in China's long history.

HOW THE WORK WAS DONE

Much planning went into the construction of this grand project. Hundreds of thousands of workers were conscripted from the southern provinces. Supply lines had to be established, a difficult task since many marauders and bandits roamed the Chinese countryside. According to one record of the period, Meng Tian established thirty-four supply bases along the Wall's proposed route, from which Wall engineers operated, as well.

Once supply bases had been established and the stream of labor began to flow into military-type construction camps, actual building commenced. Workers first built watchtowers and garrison towers, which varied in dimension, the average measuring forty feet square at the base and rising to a height of forty feet. The tower walls sloped inward, reducing the upper dimensions to about thirty feet square. Wall engineers placed such towers within sight of one another. Commonly, the distance between towers was the equivalent of two bow-shot lengths, which guaranteed that any enemy on the ground below would be within firing range of the defenders of at least one tower. Eventually, twenty-five thousand towers were completed.

The building of the Great Wall required hundreds of thousands of laborers. Here, workers lay bricks, one of the materials used to build the Wall.

The defensive role of the towers was augmented by the construction of fifteen thousand early warning outposts built on the north side of the Wall. These outposts were large enough to garrison a group of soldiers and well enough supplied to keep them self-sufficient in case of a siege. They were placed at key locations along the Wall to protect important passes, valley openings, and high-ground positions.

With construction of the towers under way, Meng Tian ordered the building of the Wall itself. The materials used in the Wall's construction varied according to the resources available in a particular region. Writer Ronald Schiller describes how this practice worked:

Architects used whatever materials were at hand to build the Wall. In rolling country and plains, it was constructed of earth and wood or carved out of natural hills, then faced and topped with stone. In deserts, the builders used layers of sand, pebbles and twigs covered with adobe bricks.

Where exactly Meng Tian began construction of his wall is uncertain, but historians believe work began in the rocky, mountainous region of eastern China. There, in solid rock, Meng's laborers dug two trenches four feet wide and twenty-five feet apart. Next, the workers laid a foundation of squared-off granite blocks in each trench to a height of six to twelve feet. Then the outer side of each wall was faced with brick. In effect, the engineers had designed a long, two-sided trough, which, like the towers, narrowed as it rose, creating a form that workers filled with rubble, stone, earth, or clay. Just as in earlier Chinese walls, built by the *hang-t'u* method, the builders tamped down this earthen filler using their feet and wooden post pounders. Bricklayers then laid down several layers of bricks on top of the rubble and compacted earth, creating a

Thousands of towers and other outposts dot the Great Wall. These structures helped make the Wall an almost impenetrable defensive line.

paved elevated roadway that could be used for protected troop movements along the border.

As the wall builders moved west, however, the terrain and available resources dictated a different method of wall construction. In the central region of China's northern provinces, workers encountered an earthen substance called loess, or in Chinese, *huangtu*, meaning yellow earth. Loess consists of very fine, yellowish brown silt. In north central China, builders found loess deposits to depths of hundreds of feet, with an underlayer of bedrock. This material soon became the primary building block in the absence of other building materials, including clay or stone.

Meng's engineers created this part of the Great Wall by slicing out sections of loess and covering them, when possible, with a brick or stone veneer. At some locations, builders reverted to the ancient tamped-earth method of wall construction, building removable wooden troughs and filling them with loess, which was then pounded hard into the form. Although the sections of Meng Tian's wall in the loess region are not as solid looking as the stone ramparts of the eastern sections, ap-

The victims of harsh weather and neglect, portions of the Wall lie in ruins. This decayed segment of wall shows the brick and earth used in its construction.

Weeds flourish in the dirt that makes up this portion of wall. As the Great Wall took shape, engineers used whatever construction materials were available, such as dirt and mud.

parently this yellow earthen material did its job well. Writing in the early twentieth century, an American adventurer named Will Geil, who had visited the Great Wall, described the loess sections of the defensive barrier:

> It has been sneeringly said the Wall in Shanxi and Gansu is only a heap of hard mud; but if mud will do to keep people out, why not use it? . . . Even now, after long neglect, when our men measured the ruins, the remains were found in many places over fifteen feet high, nearly fifteen feet thick, with towers thirty-five feet square at the base, and rising thirty feet. This would be awkward to climb over at any time, but when men are waiting on them with something . . . like boiling oil for a welcome, they would seem to furnish a good defence.

Meng's wall-building work was complicated by the antagonistic Xiongnu tribe. The Xiongnu frequently raided Meng's work camps and nearby villages from the north, forcing Meng to interrupt work on the Wall to engage in battle. In the second

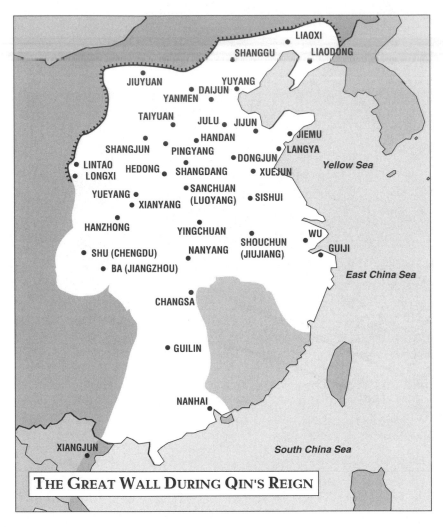

THE GREAT WALL DURING QIN'S REIGN

century B.C., a Chinese writer named Chao Cuo described the Xiongnu and the menace they posed to Meng's work. Chao's words reflect the disdain felt by the Chinese for the lifestyle of this displaced tribe:

> The Xiongnu live on meat and cheese, wear furs, and possess no house or field. They move like birds and animals in the wild. They stop only at places which abound in grass and water, want of which will start them moving again. Today, the Xiongnu are . . . waiting for a chance to make an intrusion once the garrison troops are decreased.

The Xiongnu proved a stubborn enemy. By 215 B.C., General Meng subdued the region north of the great bend in the Yellow River, where the Xiongnu had been the strongest. He ordered the construction of defensive forts along the banks of the Yellow River and in the neighboring Yinshan Mountains. Chinese historian Luo Zewen, in his book *The Great Wall of China in History and Legend*, describes the impact of Qin's new Great Wall on the Xiongnu nomads:

> After completion of the Great Wall, the Xiongnu went north for fear of Qin. They did not dare let their horses graze on southern pastures for more than 10 years. This shows that the Great Wall was significant in consolidating the unification of China and protecting the security of the Qin Empire.

Despite the tenacity of the Xiongnu, work on the Wall continued. With the completion of the Great Wall in the central loess region, the builders expanded the line of defense farther west into the Gobi Desert. Here, the evidence of Meng Tian's Wall is scant. Surviving records prove neither where this leg of the Wall was built nor how far west the Wall extended. The environment at the western end was, and still is, harsh desert, where few Chinese lived. Confusion over the exact location of the Wall in the Gobi Desert also stems from the fact that at later dates other walls were constructed at other sites in the region, several of them in close proximity to one another. Remnants of the Wall here have not weathered well, the construction being primarily that of an earthen wall. Sand deposits and wind have eroded the Wall and, in some locales, covered it completely. This final segment of the great Qin phase ends twenty-three miles west of the Chinese city of Xuzhou in the province of Kansu, two hundred miles south of the Mongolian border.

COLLAPSE OF QIN'S EMPIRE

Apart from the success of the Qin dynasty in building the Great Wall, the reign of Qin Shih Huang Ti brought much unrest throughout the empire. The Great Wall, as well as other great public works projects, had consumed the labor of hundreds of thousands of conscripted workers who were treated miserably. One primary source lamented that all along its course, "ditches on the roadside were filled with corpses of men who had been

THE DEATH OF MENG TIAN

General Meng Tian served his master, Emperor Qin Shih Huang Ti, well throughout his life. Meng oversaw the construction of his Great Wall and waged important military campaigns against the northern barbarian tribes. Meng Tian's loyalty to Qin assured Qin's favor toward him while the emperor lived. It also sealed Meng's fate when Qin died.

The emperor died in 210 B.C. while traveling far from his capital. Immediately, a plot developed to seize the throne from Qin's eldest son, Prince Fu Su. The conspiracy involved Li Si, a longtime Grand Councilor to Qin; a court eunuch named Zhao Gao; and another son of Qin's, Prince Hu Hai. Li Si understood that if Fu Su inherited the throne, he would turn to Meng Tian, whom he trusted and respected, as his new Grand Councilor, leaving Li Si without power. The three conspirators—Li Si, Zhao Gao, and Hu Hai—hatched a scheme guaranteed to bring Hu Hai to the throne.

They decided to keep Qin's death a secret by sealing the carriage carrying the dead emperor back to his court. To mask the smell of the decaying body, Zhao Gao ordered one hundred pounds of dried fish to be included in the royal procession. These fish spread an awful odor through the streets of the capital city as the emperor's carriage passed.

The conspirators then forged a letter from the emperor and sent it to Qin's heir, Prince Fu Su, and General Meng Tian, both of whom were working on the Great Wall to the north. The letter read: "As to Fu Su, who, never having done anything worthy of merit himself, yet dares to complain and speak ill of all I do; and as to Meng Tian, who has not been able to correct my son's fault during this past year: I permit them both to take their own lives." Upon receiving the letter, as tradition dictated, Prince Fu Su committed suicide.

Meng Tian, however, ordered a messenger to the capital to receive a confirmation of the order. The man did not return, however, as Li Si saw to his capture and imprisonment. Uncertain of the truth, Meng Tian hurried to the court to hear from the emperor himself. Once there, Meng Tian was taken prisoner and sentenced to die. Meng Tian responded with the following:

My family has served in Qin during three generations. With three hundred thousand men under my command, nothing could have been easier than for me to rebel. Yet I would rather die than take up arms against the imperial house. What crime have I [committed] before heaven? I die without fault.

As Meng Tian prepared himself for death by poison, the great general did feel he was guilty of *one* crime:

Indeed I have a crime for which to die. Beginning at Lintao, and extending to Liaodong, I have made ramparts and ditches over more than ten thousand *li*, and in this distance it is impossible that I have not cut through the veins of the earth. This is my crime.

Meng's words "the veins of the earth" refer to the Chinese feng shui, the belief that the earth's wind and water pass through "veins" beneath the soil, which determine the course of world events for good or ill. With these words, the faithful servant of Qin and builder of his Great Wall committed suicide.

While the death of Meng Tian seems tragic and unjustified, others living in his time did not mourn his passing. Meng Tian had proven a harsh taskmaster during his years overseeing the building of the Great Wall. A court historian named Sima Qian saw Meng's death as entirely appropriate:

What did his crime have to do with the veins of the earth? Meng Tian was a noted general, but [he did not] alleviate the distress of the common people, support the aged, care for the orphaned, or busy himself with restoring harmony among the masses. On the contrary he gave in to the ideas of the Emperor and conscripted forced labor. Is it not fitting that he . . . should meet death for this?

As for the three conspirators, their fates were soon decided. Li Si stood trial for crimes against the state, and was executed in 208. Emperor Hu Hai committed suicide that same year, convinced by Zhao Gao that the palace was under attack. Actually, the invaders were royal palace guards, disguised as rebels. But Zhao Gao met his own death in 207 when the new emperor, a son of Fu Su, ordered the assassination of the ever-conspiring and cunning court eunuch.

Visitors climb a steep portion of the Great Wall, one of China's greatest achievements.

forced into the construction of the Great Wall." In addition, the empire taxed the people of China unmercifully to pay the costs of its construction.

Qin died in 210 B.C. while visiting the coastal city of Shandong, and his empire began to crumble almost immediately. Court treachery and a contest for power followed. Because he was recognized as a threat to the new rulers of the empire, Meng Tian was ordered to commit suicide. Other Qin empire leaders were executed, and a series of rebellions erupted during the summer of 209 B.C. These peasant revolts destroyed the last remnants of the Qin dynasty. Their leaders proclaimed Qin Shih Huang Ti's rule cruel and oppressive and blamed him for death and displacement across China. The Great Wall of Qin took on a new significance. While the Wall epitomized the empire's desire to barricade itself from outsiders, it also came to represent the harsh decade of dictatorial rule of China's Only First.

3

Peace and Prosperity Along the Great Wall

For most of China's history, the Great Wall and earlier walls served as tools of war. They were erected to block invasion by outsiders and to separate warring Chinese kingdoms. During the Han dynasty, whose rulers came to power early in the third century B.C., the role of the Wall changed. For a relatively brief but important period in China's history the Chinese enjoyed peace and prosperity along the Great Wall.

The era began like most other periods in Chinese history—with warfare. Wu Di, the sixth emperor of the Han dynasty, established peaceful relations with the nomadic Xiongnu people of the north only after conquering them. But once this had been accomplished, Wu Di used the Wall to aid in expanding China's influence in the world through trade with other nations. He extended the Wall three hundred miles to the west and added a chain of watchtowers beyond the Wall's end. The Wall and watchtowers followed the route of the famed Silk Road that served as China's link to trade with the west. Although some old problems, such as Xiongnu hostility, had been solved, Wu Di took

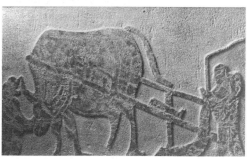

Dated to the Han dynasty, this brick design shows a pastoral agricultural scene. Under the Han, the Chinese enjoyed a period of peace and prosperity.

no chances. Many different peoples, some friendlier than others, lived on China's lengthy northern border. Thieves also posed a potential problem for traders carrying valuable goods. So Wu Di assigned thousands of soldiers to Wall outposts and watchtowers to protect the merchants and caravans traveling along the trade routes.

TRADE ALONG THE OLD SILK ROAD

A lucrative trade in all kinds of commodities soon grew between China and a variety of states to the west, including India and Parthia, later known as Persia or Iran. The northern trade route stretched across the desert lands of the T'ien Shan range. The southern road ran through the foothills of the Tibetan mountains. Both routes met at Dunhuang, a city located between the Tibetan mountains and the Mongolian desert. There the two roads split, then reconnected a thousand miles west of Dunhuang at Kashgar, located today in the modern Chinese region of Sinkiang. Here the two roads split once more, traveling through what is now Afghanistan. Chinese traders went no farther west, but trade between the Chinese and the Parthians did not end there. The Parthians served as middlemen between the Chinese and traders on the continent of Europe. Historian Robert Silverberg describes just how extensive and important trade along the Silk Road was to all those involved:

> Along the silk roads went camel caravans, winding past snow-topped mountains and parched deserts. Merchants carried spices, furs, silks, and porcelains out of China and returned with wool, linen, glass, precious stones, gold, jade, fine horses, skilled craftsmen, and such exotic foods as raisins. The Parthians were middlemen in this trade. They did business with Rome and Syria, and with China as well. The goods of East and

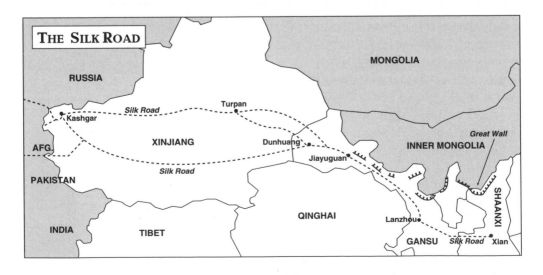

This structure along the Silk Road—now in ruins—must have bustled with activity during its heyday.

West were exchanged in the market places of Parthia, and Chinese merchants mingled with travelers from Rome.

EMPEROR WU DI'S WALL

Much of Wu Di's Wall was built in the *hang-t'u* style of pounded earth. Builders placed layers of reed in several sections to give the Wall additional support much as modern builders suspend steel rods in concrete to strengthen and stabilize such modern structures. Historian-writer Luo Zewen describes the process in the building of the Han Wall:

> In desert areas walls were built of reeds and tamarisk [a desert shrub] twigs layered with sand. . . . First a layer of reeds or tamarisk branches, then a layer of sand, then another layer of reeds or tamarisk branches, until the wall reached 5 to 6 meters [16 to 19 feet].

A series of unconnected watchtowers stretched nearly seventy miles west of Dunhuang, the Wall's western terminus. Erected within sight of one another, the towers made up an early warning system in case of attack. Those manning these

THE WESTERN EXPEDITION OF ZHANG QIAN

Prior to the reign of Emperor Wu Di, no Chinese citizen on record had ever traveled to the remote western lands beyond Jiayuguan, the traditional end of the Great Wall. However, to explore the possibilities of extending Chinese influence into this barbarous land, Wu Di sent a young military officer named Zhang Qian into the region.

Emperor Wu Di had instructed Zhang to make contact with a western tribe of barbarians called the Yuezhi. This barbarian tribe had been driven west by the Xiongnu less than a decade after the fall of Qin Shih Huang Ti's empire, around the year 200 B.C. Wu Di hoped Zhang would be able to convince the Yuezhi to unite with the Chinese and join them in their struggle against the Xiongnu.

Zhang Qian left on his trek of discovery in 138 B.C., in the company of about one hundred soldiers. Unfortunately, once the party moved beyond the protection of the Great Wall, Zhang and his men were captured by the Xiongnu. Their captivity lasted for ten years, until Zhang Qian escaped with some of his followers. However, rather than return to the emperor as a failure, he continued his journey west, still in search of the elusive Yuezhi. His travels took him far to the west to the city of Ferghana. There he received news that the tribe he was searching for had migrated to the southwest.

Once he finally caught up with the Yuezhi, he began his negotiations. Yet the Yuezhi were not interested in uniting with the Chinese. In fact, their own migrations had put them at considerable distance from both the Chinese and the Xiongnu. After living with them for a year, Zhang Qian left the Yuezhi and began his long trip back to China. His return was interrupted when he was captured a second

outposts could signal to the next tower in case of trouble and the message could then make its way quickly back to Dunhuang. Hungarian-born archaeologist Mark Aurel Stein discovered one of these watchtowers during excavations in 1907. The remains of the ancient fortress measured fifteen feet on a side, rising to a height of twenty-three feet. Clay bricks reinforced with tamarisk twigs were used to build the time by the Xiongnu. This time, however, they only held him for a year.

At last, Zhang Qian returned to China. The expedition had faced many trials and suffered many deaths. Only one of his hundred men remained, a servant named Ganfu. While Zhang failed in his efforts to enlist the Yuezhi against the Xiongnu, he brought back with him tales of many adventures. In addition, he returned to the court of the emperor with a large collection of exotic animals he discovered in the west, as well as a great collection of plants previously unknown to the Chinese.

Among his stories, Zhang told about the great wealth he had seen in the west. He spoke about India, describing a state "low, damp, and hot, and the people ride on elephants to fight in battle." He described great trade routes. Zhang talked about the territory around Ferghana and of the people there, who "have grapevines and many excellent horses. These are blood-sweating horses whose stock is the offspring of the Heavenly Horses."

Emperor Wu Di was so impressed by Zhang Qian's stories that he set his mind and his foreign policy westward. He began to expand his influence to the west, seeking riches, trade, and contacts. He launched an all-out campaign against the Xiongnu, defeating them in 119 B.C. In a few years, Wu Di's influence was well established in the far-flung western lands. China began trading along the route that became known as the Old Silk Road. Chinese embassies were built in the west. As Chinese involvement in the trade of the Old Silk Road became a major element of the empire's economy, Wu Di extended the Great Wall hundreds of miles west of Jiayuguan. All this as a result of the great expedition of Zhang Qian.

tower. Inside the ruins, Stein uncovered several artifacts, including, according to his written records, "a piece of wool, fragments of iron tools, and a few scraps of carved wood." Continuing his search for Han-era structures, Stein uncovered other towers, many of them well preserved. Each featured an elevated platform on which soldiers stood watch, with a short parapet providing protection. From these

Towers and other structures line this stretch of crumbling, decayed wall. Although now militarily obsolete, the structures once housed soldiers who guarded the Wall against enemy assault.

ramparts, signal fires could be lit to warn guards down the line of an approaching enemy.

Written records uncovered by Stein and others have revealed many details of the life of soldiers garrisoned along the Han Wall. A typical garrison included an arsenal of crossbows and javelins, as well as an array of torches, flares, signal flags, and domestic items such as cooking utensils. Those guarding the Wall used an elaborate system of signals involving everything from flags to smoke and fire to communicate with towers up and down the line.

Some watchtowers made use of Wall watchdogs. In some places, sand deposits were smoothed adjacent to the north side of the Wall. Each morning, the guards emerged into barbarian territory, inspecting the sand for tracks and other evidence of enemy movement. Border dogs often accompanied such patrols.

Of his discoveries in the western desert, Stein writes:

Never did I realize more deeply how little two thousand years mean where human activity is suspended, and even that of Nature benumbed, than when on my long reconnoitering rides the evenings found me along at some commanding watch-station. Struck by the rays of the setting sun tower after tower, up to ten miles' distance or more, could be seen glittering as if the plaster coating which their walls had once carried was still intact. . . . How easy it was then to imagine that towers and wall were still guarded and that watchful eyes were scanning the deceptive depressions northward for that fleet and artful enemy, the Huns.

MILITARY LIFE ALONG THE GREAT WALL

During the Han dynasty, the soldiers who manned the garrisons of the Great Wall of China were mostly conscripted recruits, drafted into military duty along the border. Generally, they served in small units, living and working in the watchtowers of the Wall. Not all their work in the far-off stations was military in nature, however. Often these border recruits farmed nearby plots, the produce from which made the garrisons more self-sufficient. Grain and crop harvests were stored in storage

An elaborate system of signals developed so that soldiers garrisoned along the Wall could communicate with one another.

bins sometimes as large as 150 feet by 500 feet. Rations were allocated according to the guards' age, their rank, and whether or not their families lived nearby.

The towers were sturdy structures built almost entirely of brick, covered with a thick coat of whitewashed plaster. Michael Loewe, in his book *Everyday Life in Early Imperial China*, describes a typical interior:

> Some of [the towers] boasted several rooms, whose doors were fitted with bolts to secure privacy. Some towers rose to a height of five to ten meters [sixteen to thirty-two feet], with a stairway or ladder that provided access to the top. This was laid out as a platform and surrounded by crenellated walls so as to afford maximum protection to the defence. Heavy crossbows were hung on the walls, their quivers stiff with arrows, and there were sighting devices with which to direct the shooting accurately. Defensive armour and helmets were provided, and there were supplies of grease and glue for the care and maintenance of weapons. At some sites a pole was erected for hoisting signals, and each tower kept flags, or torches, for the purpose. For their daily needs the men stored their water in jars, and they may have been able to convey it in earthenware pipes. There was a brazier stoked with dung on which the section's cooking-pot simmered, and some of the posts were equipped with medicine chests.

In addition to their military duties, some border soldiers also worked as customs agents. In border communities closest to the Silk Road, where foreigners were common, those passing from one side of the Wall to the other submitted to a checkpoint search. Guards examined the necessary papers qualifying travelers to enter China, much like border officials check tourists' passports today. Border guards also examined the goods travelers carried, looking for contraband. Border stations kept very detailed records of the comings and goings of those passing through the gates of the Great Wall.

INTERNATIONAL TRADE

When Emperor Wu Di died in 87 B.C., the era of peace and prosperity along the Wall did not end. Although later Han rulers were weaker than Wu Di, and their reigns were beset by intrigue and assassination, peace and trade along the Wall continued.

Over time, the trade between the Chinese and the Xiongnu, their northern neighbors, grew extensive. One Chinese record from 81 B.C. described the important elements of this new international border trade:

> A piece of Chinese plain silk can be exchanged with the Xiongnu for articles worth several pieces of gold. . . . Mules, donkeys, and camels enter the frontier in unbroken lines; horses, dapples and bays, and prancing mounts come into our possession. The furs of sables, marmots, foxes, and badgers, colored rugs and decorated carpets fill the imperial treasury, while jade and auspicious stones, corals, and crystals become national treasures. That is to say, foreign products keep flowing in, while our wealth is not dissipated. National wealth not being dispersed abroad, the people enjoy abundance.

Such trade helped bring to China a new level of prosperity and security. No longer did the Xiongnu represent the ferocious foe of the past. They were trading partners, and the Great Wall served as the portal of commerce and venue of cultural exchange rather than the barrier of defense. Marriages were contracted between the two peoples, eventually including those of Chinese princesses and barbarian Xiongnu husbands.

A TEMPTING OFFER

The close relationship between the Chinese and the Xiongnu continued until, in 33 B.C., the Chinese received an offer from their neighbors. A Xiongnu *shan-yu*, or chief, named Khujanga, as a gesture of friendship, actually proposed to the Chinese emperor, Yuan Ti, that the Xiongnu take over control of the Great Wall. Khujanga pledged to the emperor that his people would be responsible for the upkeep of the Wall and for the general security of the northern borderlands.

When the offer reached the Han court, many Chinese officials trusted the sincerity of Khujanga's offer and encouraged the emperor to accept it. The cost of maintaining and garrisoning the Wall had always been a drain on the Chinese government's resources. Here was an offer that was, indeed, tempting. At one point, Emperor Yuan Ti was prepared to accept it. However, an aged minister of the Han court spoke up against the proposal:

> Since the time of Chou [Zhou] and Ch'in [Qin] the encroachment of the Xiongnu upon our territories has been of frequent occurrence . . . until Emperor Wu defeated them utterly, driving them north into the desert and reinforcing the whole length of the Great Wall.

> Besides serving as a bulwark against invaders, the frontier posts are kept on constant guard to stop the escape of traitors from our own country. Many of the subjects of northernmost China are descendants of barbarians, and therefore have to be watched extremely carefully if treachery is to be avoided. The Great Wall was built more than a century ago. It is not a mere mud rampart. Up hill and down dale it follows the natural contours of the earth. It is riddled with many secret underground passages, and watch-towers with slit windows provide strategically placed lookouts from which our archers can cover the surrounding hills.

The wise old counselor concluded his speech with a warning that ultimately convinced the emperor that the offer, though tempting, should be turned down: "If we dispense with these fortifications China's safety would depend entirely upon the goodwill of the Xiongnu chieftains, whose ambitions would surely lead to annexation of part of our land." The Xiongnu offer was refused.

"THE OVER-ENTERPRISING CHINESE"

Emperor Yuan Ti let his ally down gently by writing how pleased he was to "learn that you would be prepared to take over from our forces the defence of our frontiers as a token of [your] loyalty." However, the emperor added,

> The Flower Kingdom [China], as supreme arbiter of the Universe, possesses frontiers other than those to the north, and Our armies not only have to resist aggression

from outside, but hold back Our people from invading the territory of friendly neighbors. Know then that the Great Wall was built not so much to protect the Empire against the outer world, as to protect the outer world from the over-enterprising Chinese.

THE END OF THE HAN EMPIRE

The days of the Han were numbered as foreign enemies mounted increasing attacks and old feudal families within the empire began to rebel. Finally, in A.D. 220, the Han empire fell. Weak provincial rulers attempted localized rule in the absence of central authority, but so ineffective were many of these leaders that the Great Wall fell into barbarian hands by 300. The Wall was neglected and portions fell into disrepair.

In time, barbarian tribes filtered south of the Wall and took control of China. Once in power, several new rulers began making repairs on the Wall. Various barbarian emperors over a three-hundred-year period ordered the construction of more than a thousand miles of new walls, most designed to keep other northern tribes from overrunning China and ending their dynasties.

Despite the rebuilding and new construction, the era of peace and prosperity along the Wall had ended.

The emperor of the Tang dynasty receives visitors. The rise of the Tang dynasty marked a period when the Great Wall fell into disuse and, ultimately, disrepair.

The Wall's significance was also diminished. With the rise of the Tang dynasty, beginning in 618, the military strategy of the Chinese turned to offensive tactics, rather than defensive measures. The walls constructed prior to the seventh century A.D. had no place in such a strategy. Guard towers were abandoned and the walls crumbled. Even after the collapse of the Tang dynasty in 906, four centuries would pass before the Great Wall regained a prominent place in China's affairs.

4

THE MING DYNASTY REBUILDS

By the time the Ming dynasty rose to power in 1368, the Great Wall had lost all of its majesty. Much of its three-thousand-mile span had fallen into disrepair during four hundred years of neglect. Guard towers took on a tumbledown look. Weeds pried the Wall's stones apart. Northern barbarian tribes had breached the Wall in dozens of places, leaving great gaps in the ancient structure. But the Ming, who ruled from 1368–1644, gave new life to China's Wall. The Ming pursued the most serious wall-building policy to date. Over a period of two hundred years, through the reigns of nearly a dozen emperors, the Ming restored the entire Wall, added to its length, and fortified it more than had any previous rulers. The traditional northern barrier became a formidable defense, manned by one million men and kept in a state of military readiness for century after century of Ming rule. Herein lies the true legacy of the Great Wall of China. Historian Robert Silverberg describes the impact of the Ming on the history of the Great Wall:

> The Great Wall was now taking the shape it has today. It had become a solid brick rampart topped by elegant battlements and parapets. Along the mountains north of Peking there ran the finest section of all, twenty-five feet thick at the base, fifteen to thirty feet high, fifteen feet across at the top. The Ming emperors spared no effort to keep that part of the Wall in perfect shape.

The Ming dynasty's devotion to restoring and extending the Wall grew out of a fierce determination to free China from the threat of foreign domination. For about 150 years before the Ming rose to power, China had been subject to rule by the Mongolian people of the north. Mongol leader Genghis Khan came to power in 1215 and established the ruling Yuan dynasty, which continued with Genghis Khan's grandson Kublai Khan, who declared himself emperor of all China. Although life for the Chinese changed little under Mongolian rule, the Chinese despised foreign domination. With Kublai Khan's death in 1294, the Chinese saw their chance to regain control of their land.

For the next seventy years, rebel forces mounted small-scale attacks, and scattered unrest undermined Mongol authority. Then, under the leadership of a former monk named Zhu Yuanzhang, a general uprising pushed the Mongols and their Yuan dynasty out of China and their capital at Beijing. Once again, the northern barbarians found themselves on the other side of the Great Wall. In 1368, Zhu Yuanzhang became the first emperor of a new Chinese rule, the Ming dynasty.

Despite Zhu Yuanzhang's success in removing the Mongolian influence from China, the Mongols presented a continuing threat, repeatedly attempting to regain their hold over northern

The legendary Mongol leader Genghis Khan founded the Yuan dynasty when he came to power in China in 1215.

GENGHIS KHAN: EMPEROR OF ALL MEN

The exploits of Genghis Khan are legendary. Born between 1155 and 1167, his given name was Temujin. As an adult warrior he brought various nomadic peoples together and launched a campaign to conquer as much of the territory of central Asia as possible. By 1206, he had taken the title of Genghis Khan, which is translated as Emperor of All Men, or Greatest of Rulers. Under his leadership, the Mongols conquered province after province, defeating many other rulers, including those of the Jin empire in northern China.

For the Khan, the Great Wall was no impenetrable barrier. He was able to breach the Wall in several places, failing only in his 1211 campaign to take the capital city of Yanjing, where he broke through the old Wall but could not storm the gates of the city, with their forty-foot-high walls and guard towers manned by crossbow-firing soldiers. However, Genghis Khan returned four years later, after tightening his grasp over additional Chinese provinces, and saw to the defeat of Yanjing in 1215. Until his death in 1227, Genghis Khan expanded his military conquests throughout not only China, but central Asia, as well. His followers simply continued their exploits after their great leader's death, overrunning everything in their path, their empire stretching from Korea in the east to Turkey in the west.

The legacy of Genghis Khan continued through his grandson, Kublai Khan, who became the Mongol emperor in 1260. Kublai Khan consolidated Mongolian control over China, creating the Yuan dynasty. He died in 1294 but not until he witnessed the development of a dynasty that was strong "militarily and economically" and that had created "considerable achievements in science and the arts." However, the Chinese under his rule took little comfort in Kublai Khan's successes. Despite all the civilizing influences China had to offer the Mongols, they nevertheless remained, in the eyes of the Chinese, foreigners and outsiders.

China. Keeping them out became an all-important goal of the Ming rulers, who understood the necessity of reestablishing an unassailable military defense. Ming rulers were constantly reminded of this necessity by their military leaders in the field. Typical advice, this from a noted Chinese writer of the day, Wei Huan, went as follows:

Kublai Khan declared himself emperor of China in the thirteenth century. Although he was a tolerant ruler, the Chinese despised foreign domination.

> The minorities in north China who lead a nomadic life, and excel at horsemanship and marksmanship, often attack and plunder the border areas, coming and going unpredictably. In the past dynasties troops were stationed there to guard the frontiers. We must make use of natural barriers such as mountains and rivers. Man-made barriers ought to be set up along the strategically important terrains. Our country has driven away the intruders . . . and is now unified. To hold our land together, we should set up a series of strategic posts—*zhen*—and station troops at each.

Re-Creating the Great Wall

Zhu Yuanzhang took the warnings to heart. He embarked on a massive rebuilding campaign and reinforced troops all along the Wall. Zhu Yuanzhang (who reigned as Hung-wu) even sent nine of his sons to the north to serve as garrison commanders along the Great Wall.

William Edgar Geil, in *The Great Wall of China*, explains that the remilitarization of the Wall was immediate and serious:

> At each transit pass capable of admitting carts and horsemen, guard posts of one hundred men each were established. At the smaller passes for carriers of fuel and herdsmen with their flocks, ten men. The instructions given to the generals ran thus: "At each signal station let the towers be built higher and stronger; within must be laid up food, fuel, medicine, and weapons for four moons. Beside the tower let a wall be

opened, enclosed by a wall as high as the tower itself, presenting the appearance of a double gateway, inner and outer. Be on your guard at all times with anxious care." Such were the commands of the Emperor.

During the reign of the third Ming ruler, Zhu Di, who ruled under the name Yung-lo, the necessity of protecting and re-building the Great Wall took on a new urgency. In 1421, late in his reign, Zhu Di returned the capital of China from Nanking in the south, where Zhu Yuanzhang had moved it, to Beijing. This was a significant step: The seat of the Ming empire was now a mere twelve miles from the Great Wall itself, and ex-tremely close to the barbarians of the north. The Wall once again became the first line of defense for the emperor, the Chi-nese people, and their way of life.

An excerpt from the official history of the Ming reveals just why the Great Wall became, once again, a major instrument of Chinese foreign policy:

In 1421, Ming ruler Zhu Di moved the capital of China from Nanking to Beijing, situated only twelve miles from the Great Wall. (Below) The museum popularly known as the Forbidden City was once the imperial palace of the Ming dy-nasty. (Left) A close-up of the sea dragons that line the roof of the For-bidden City shows the artistry of Chinese architecture.

This beautiful marble arch and the portion of wall it penetrates were built during the Yuan dynasty.

Once they had been driven out of China, the descendants of the Yuan dynasty (the Mongols) constantly endeavored to regain their lost domain. When [Yung-lo] moved the capital up north, the Great Wall was close by on three sides but the enemy became daily more troublesome. The defense of the Great Wall therefore became of leading importance as the Ming Dynasty wore on.

The Great Wall of China under the Ming was generally constructed south of the Wall built during the reign of Qin Shih Huang Ti. Many of the Qin ramparts had fallen apart, their earthen walls eroded by centuries of neglect and harsh weather. Just as Qin had relied on Meng Tian, various Ming emperors relied on several of their generals to oversee reconstruction on the Great Wall. In some cases, military governors were held responsible for the rebuilding in their districts.

MATERIALS USED ON THE MING WALL

The materials used in the original Wall construction were generally procured locally. Everything from stone blocks, wooden timbers, glazed tiles, and lots of fill dirt was put to use in building the earlier walls. Much of the work on the Ming Wall involved

Ming builders used not only materials they could find, such as dirt and stones, but they also advanced technology to create better, stronger walls. Here, Chinese laborers shape bricks that will be fired in the kiln.

similar materials but advanced technology on a grander scale. Quarries were tapped for stones. Bricks were formed on-site and fired in kilns built near the Wall. Forest crews were sent into the northern woods to chop down oaks, pines, and firs, and saw them into usable planks. The lumber was used to rebuild watch-towers and garrison buildings. If timber was not available lo-cally, then workers hauled the wood from a distance.

Building materials were transported to the various work sites along the course of the Great Wall by several means. First and foremost, hundreds of thousands of men and women were used as bearers, forced to carry on their backs everything from sawn timbers to bricks and mortar. Sometimes, especially when the route led uphill, workers formed a line and handed bricks and other building materials from person to person.

Such human conveyor belts might extend for miles over steep mountain ranges. Sometimes, on flat terrain, peasant workers pushed small handcarts capable of carrying stones weighing over a hundred pounds. In addition, workers depended on various tools including levers and windlasses, simple hoisting systems of ropes and cranks used to raise and lower loads. These

Ming dynasty workers fill baskets at the bottom of the Wall. At the top, a crank-driven instrument moves the baskets to the top, where the contents will be dropped and used for construction. The baskets continue their circular journey to the bottom of the Wall, where the process repeats itself.

basic machines made the positioning of very heavy stones possible. Illustrations from the late Ming dynasty show workers using a contraption that looks like a conveyor belt of baskets. The crank-driven apparatus moved filled baskets to the top of the Wall, automatically dumped their loads, and then returned them to the bottom to be filled again. Workers also suspended heavy loads in baskets at both ends of a wooden rod balanced across their shoulders.

Pack animals provided another means of transport for all kinds of materials. The Chinese relied primarily on donkeys and goats to carry loads that might include bricks, stones, earthen fill, and lime. Some surviving illustrations show donkeys with baskets strapped to their sides, loaded with bricks. Workers also tied bricks to the horns of goats, then drove them up steep mountain inclines.

MING BUILDING METHODS

Much of the Ming Great Wall was brickwork, which required thousands of masons and semiskilled laborers. Modern writer-historian Luo Zewen describes the brick wall–building process:

> The Wall at Juyongguan and Badaling near Beijing snakes its way through the mountains. A closer look shows that stone slabs which serve as the bedrock of each layer of bricks are parallel. The brick battlements on the wall were also built layer upon layer. Flights of stairway were used to compensate for the variation in elevation. The outer and inner sides of the thick wall were faced with stone slabs, and then stones, cobbles, lime, and earth were stuffed in between. When the slabs and land-fill reached the prescribed height, bricks were laid on top, complete with battlements and parapets.

In places, the top brick layer formed flights of stairs as the undulating Wall followed slopes of more than forty-five degrees.

In addition to brick construction, builders also relied on earthen walls. Unlike earlier earthen walls built in three- to four-inch layers, the Ming walls were constructed of earthen layers eight inches thick.

The Ming rulers were intent on fortifying their Great Wall above all others. Portions were built along narrow mountain

JUYONGGUAN PASS: GUARDIAN OF BEIJING

Forty miles outside of Beijing, China's present-day capital and the capital of the Ming rulers of the fourteenth and fifteenth centuries, lies Juyongguan Pass. This place—along with its well-fortified Mount Badaling—is one of the best preserved fortress sites along the Wall.

The pass is actually a valley cutting its way through the Jundu Mountains, where the town of Nankou stands today. Here the Wall and its beacon towers lie in ruin. Six miles away stands a series of forts on the summit of Mount Badaling, entered by two main gates. The western gate bears the inscription "Lock of the North Entrance." On the eastern gate are the words "Frontline before Juyongguan."

A portion of the Wall at Mount Badaling shows its undulating course through the mountain.

Juyongguan Pass and Mount Badaling were greatly prized by the Ming. Here the Wall snakes and dips up and down mountain walls, appearing and reappearing, presenting to all would-be invaders a harsh and impregnable defense line like no other on earth.

ridges, which in themselves presented a natural barrier to an outside enemy. The Wall extended over topography ranging from mountains to plateaus, rivers to deserts, grasslands to swamps. Towers were built at regular intervals, along narrow mountain passes, at the bend of a river, or at crossroads. Many towers were located on high ground, so that the flames and smoke of signal fires could be seen from greater distances, and so that fewer bricks were needed for already high ramparts. In *The Great Wall of China in History and Legend*, writers Luo Zewen and Zhao Luo describe how the Ming builders used the natural terrain for their own purposes:

> For instance, the Badaling wall near Juyongguan was built along a mountain ridge. The ridge made the wall steeper and harder to attack. In some places the slope is

Builders used bricks to form flights of stairs where segments of wall followed steep upward slopes.

very steep on the outside but relatively flat inside, because the outside was for blocking the enemy, whereas the inside was for the guards to walk about. Huge rocks and cliffs were already fit for fortifications, needing only a few changes. Where there were precipitous cliffs, the wall would stop, for the cliffs were fortifications in themselves.

Yet while the primary goal of the builders and designers of the Ming Wall was to create a well-fortified bastion, the architects and builders managed to make the Wall beautiful, as well. Again, historian Luo Zewen writes in *The Great Wall:*

> The wall owes its beauty to these [engineers and architects]. For they created the most diverse styles of towers and gates, in beautiful architectural proportions, and often furnished with artistic decoration that from the military viewpoint could only be said to have been

superfluous. Such, for instance, is the case with Ji-ayuguan Fort, which lies far out in the wilderness, and its magnificent East Gate, where the tower is decorated with rich wood carvings on its columns and rafters, and the roof is worthy of a temple. The same may be said of Shanhaiguan at the other end of the wall, and of many garrisons, castles, and passes which lie in between.

The architects demonstrated their decorative abilities in the building of other structures near the Wall itself. Not only defense towers but elaborate small temples (for the worship of Guandi, the god of war) and shrines were built, along with teahouses and other sacred buildings.

After completing construction on these martial monuments, the builders frequently signed their names to the Wall, creating dedication stones in which were inscribed the name of the

Although the Wall was built primarily as a defense against invaders, its architects managed to create a monument of lasting beauty.

local builder and the date on which that section of wall was completed. The following is a typical example of this pride of workmanship:

General of the Light Brigade, Zui Jing,
Commanding the Yeomanry
under the jurisdiction of the Governor by Imperial
Appointment at Paoting.
Ensign Shen Zixian of the above Department,
Ensign Sun Er-huo, Superintendent of Works,
Liu Jing, Military Contractor,
and others to the number of 130 names
cooperated in building this extension of 591 feet,
6 inches of Third Class Wall,
beginning in the north at the end of the
Military Graduate Long Guangxian's portion of
Tower No. 55
of the Black Letter 'Wu' series.

The appeal of the Great Wall is truly timeless; visitors continue to be thrilled by its seemingly endless, twisting course that weaves through the natural terrain.

The completion of the construction was reported by the
Autumn Guard
on the 16th day of the 9th moon of the 4th Year of
Wanli.
Master Stonemason Zhao Yanmei and others.
Master Border Artisan Lu Huan and others.

But perhaps the most aesthetically pleasing element of the
design of the Great Wall is its twisting, almost meandering
course. The defensive structure weaves a path across the
mountains, dipping from sight, only to rise again on some distant hillock. Its seemingly endless course provides the natural
Chinese landscape with a man-made ornament, a twisting
necklace of stone and brick that enhances and further mystifies
an already dramatic and mysterious place.

5

WANLI'S LONG WALL

After decades of toil by thousands of workers, the Great Wall of the Ming dynasty was firmly established, becoming the primary symbol of Ming power. An anonymous Portuguese visitor to China, writing in the late 1550s, left this account:

> At the boundary of the kingdom of China, where it borders on the Tartars, there is a wall of wondrous strength, of a month's journey in extent, where the king keeps a great military force in the bulwarks [fortresses]. Where this wall comes upon mountains, they cut them in such a manner that they remain and serve as a wall; for the Tartars are very brave and skillful in war. . . . A strict watch is kept on the wall.

The reinforced Wall was a fortification like no other before it in China's history. Yet the Ming were not finished with their work on the great barrier.

THE EMPEROR WANLI

Just a few years after the Portuguese traveler recorded his impressions, the Ming emperor whose name is most closely connected with the building of the Ming Great Wall rose to the throne. His name was Zhuyijun. Assuming the title of emperor and the royal name of Wanli in 1572, this thirteenth ruler in the Ming dynastic line, and the last powerful ruler of the empire, occupied the throne for forty-eight years. The restorations he ordered on the Wall were so extensive that for centuries after his death people in China believed the Wall was begun during his reign. The common Chinese name for the Wall, Wanli Aiang Zheng, translates as Wall of Ten Thousand Miles; it is often translated as Wanli's Long Wall. This last of the great Ming rulers created for himself a grand legacy in rebuilding and extending the Wall.

Much of the Great Wall in existence today dates from the reign of Wanli. He ordered repair work and an extension of the

Wall west of the Yellow River, and repaired sections in the east that had been neglected by earlier Ming rulers. The emperor's name often shows up on repaired as well as new sections. Typical is the following record of progress on the Wall: "two pieces of First Class Wall, each piece 148 tens of feet long plus eight feet, in the Lucky Days of the Winter Season in the Third Year of Wanli."

Much of the work completed under the Emperor Wanli represented Chinese craftsmanship at its best. Historian Robert Silverberg describes some of the work completed under Wanli's orders:

> The excellently preserved section of the Wall at the Nankou Pass, long a tourist favorite, dates mainly from this reign, though there has been some restoration since Wanli's time. Here, the Wall is built of granite blocks accurately cut and dressed; some of the blocks are fourteen feet long and three or four feet thick. The upper part of the Wall is brick, and the brick is of high quality.

This section of wall at Nankou Pass draws thousands of tourists each year. This view shows the huge granite blocks from which Wanli's Wall is constructed.

At fifty-foot intervals along the 14-foot-wide roadway the Ming builders installed stone drains to carry rain water out of the roadbed, letting it pour onto the Mongol side of the Wall. This architectural refinement has had a considerable effect in preserving the Wall at that point.

Earlier Great Wall designers had not accounted for heavy rains along much of its course. Previous Wall construction allowed rain to seep behind the Wall's stones and masonry. Frequently such water deposits froze in winter, causing cracks and fissures in the Wall's exterior. The stone drains built by the Ming helped prevent such deterioration.

DEFENDING THE DEFENSE

Emperor Wanli used the Great Wall much as earlier Ming rulers had. His wall was part of a greatly fortified and heavily guarded complex. This system of walls, fortresses, and garrisons provided protection for the empire. However, Wanli's Wall represented not only a massive stone, brick, and earthen barrier, but a formidable force comprising soldiers on the Wall itself, local military units along the lines of a local militia or home guard, and regional centers of government, which shared responsibility with the emperor for protecting local divisions of the Great Wall.

On a regional level, responsibility for the Wall was allocated to military zones called *zhen*. Originally, four *zhen* were established; eventually, five more were added. Each *zhen* was commanded by a general and had its own headquarters, usually located in a city near the Wall or in a strategically placed fort.

Each *zhen* was subdivided into *lu*, commanded by an officer analogous to a modern-day garrison commander. Above both the *zhen* and *lu* commanders was the office of chairman of a province or a minister of the central government, a figure who usually administered several *zhen*.

Locally, the basic units of defense were garrisons built along the Wall, each of which included several companies of border guards numbering one hundred or more. These companies lived along the Wall in structures called castles. Each castle had its own beacon tower as a primary means of commu-

DEFENDERS IN ACTION

The troops of the Great Wall were among the best equipped of all Ming dynasty soldiers, and their garrisons bristled with an array of shields, swords, crossbows, halberds (a battle-ax and pike on a six-foot pole), and even artillery.

A typical soldier wore a lightweight suit of wicker and leather armor into battle either on the Wall or on the ground. Properly armed Wall defenders selected from a variety of bladed weapons, such as lances and axes, and sledge hammers were used along the ramparts. Defenders mounted large crossbows on sawhorse-type platforms that could fire an iron bolt at an enemy from a distance of "two hundred long paces." Ground reinforcements often rode horses with leather armor and even spears extending along their flanks to impale slow-moving enemy troops. Soldiers entering battle not only brandished their weapons, but carried flags, blew trumpets, beat drums to frighten the barbarians, and shouted in unison on command. One such command barked by an officer to his unit ordered his men to "Look frightening now!"

nication with others up and down the Wall. The number of soldiers stationed at each castle varied according to the strategic significance of each fortress. The garrisons at Jiayuguan and Shanhaiguan Passes, for example, often numbered nearly one thousand men.

SHANHAIGUAN PASS

Shanhaiguan Pass was an important link in the Great Wall. It was the easternmost line of defense. Here the mountain chains dip to sea level, providing a possible point where invaders might easily slip into China.

Shanhaiguan became a key fortress along the Ming Wall. A castle fortification was built there in 1381. The fortress is massive, its four walls totaling over two miles in length. A moat surrounds the fortress, measuring more than fifty feet across and twenty feet deep. Additional garrisons, forts, and beacon towers—some in ruins today—stood outside this extensive inner fortress. One such additional fortress, Ninghai Castle, stands at the actual site where the Great Wall rises out of the waters of Bohai Bay, beginning the Wall in the east.

JIAYUGUAN PASS

At the western end of the Ming Wall, thousands of miles from Shanhaiguan, stood the fortress at Jiayuguan Pass. South of the pass rise the Qilian Mountains. To the north is the Gobi Desert. Construction on its castle-fortress began in 1372. The walls in this region were built in the *hang-t'u* method of rammed earth. Here, as at Shanhaiguan, invaders faced an inviting route into China. Therefore, the Ming fortified the site heavily.

Coauthors Luo Zewen and Zhao Luo describe the castle and its defensive position at Jiayuguan:

> The pass is shaped like a trapezoid, big at the west end and small at the east. The east wall is about 154 meters [approximately 500 feet] long, the west about 166 meters [544 feet], the north and south about 160 meters [524 feet]. Outside the west wall there is another thick wall, making the defence in the west particularly solid. Another low rammed-earth wall starts from the western end of the outer wall and encircles the pass, paralleling

A fortress at Jiayuguan marks the western end of the Great Wall. Heavy fortifications at Jiayuguan kept many invaders from entering China.

Another view of Jiayuguan Pass shows why the western end of the Ming Wall thwarted would-be invaders.

the south and north walls. To the east of the pass another rammed-earth wall encloses a square. Outside the castle wall, there are also triangular snares for trapping horses.

Additional defensive measures are evident at Jiayuguan. Two-story brick towers mark the castle's four corners. Watchtowers flank the southern and northern walls. A heavily armed garrison of troops lived inside the castle. Barracks and storage buildings provided sleeping quarters and housed the equipment needed for the fort. Weapons used to arm the troops at Jiayuguan included "armour, bows and arrows, and big guns of the Ming." Thirty-nine beacon towers line the Wall at Jiayuguan. The combination of walled fortifications, towers, signal sites, and a thousand well-armed soldiers kept many invaders from targeting Jiayuguan as their point of entry into imperial China.

BUTTRESSES AND RAMPARTS

Soldiers who patrolled at Shanhaiguan, Jiayuguan, or any number of other forts scattered along the Great Wall were aided by such architectural features as buttresses and ramparts. Buttresses were blockhouses that jutted out from the

Wall at regular intervals, where troops could store equipment and gain access to stations atop the Wall. Engineers had designed buttresses as protection from an enemy firing arrows from below. They included holes, or crenellations, through which Wall guards could fire on invaders attempting to scale the Wall. When not serving a military purpose, the buttresses provided places where soldiers on duty could rest.

The Wall's architectural features aided the soldiers who guarded China's borders. For example, this section of Wanli's Wall includes crenellations, or holes, through which guards could fire on invaders.

Ramparts were equally important to Wall defense. A rampart is an embankment of the Wall itself, rising two or three stories above the running course of the Wall. Ramparts provided the garrisoned soldiers a place to live and to store their weapons and provisions. Their original designer was a Ming-era general named Qi Jiguang, who served Emperor Wanli. In his book *Records of Military Training*, Qi Jiguang gives rampart dimensions of thirty to forty feet in height and forty to sixty yards square. Typically, they were built at intervals of approximately three hundred feet at strategic locations and six hundred to nine hundred feet on foothills and flatlands. Each rampart had to be in sight of its two adjacent ramparts so that one could easily signal the next in case of an enemy's approach. Ramparts, built on level ground, extended about sixteen feet into foreign territory and approximately six feet into the Chinese side. On top of the rampart was a tower where soldiers could station themselves, armed with crossbows or, in later years, small cannon. A typical rampart garrisoned between thirty and fifty soldiers.

SIGNALING THE ALARM: BEACON TOWERS

The primary duty of soldiers stationed along the Wall was to observe the approach of an enemy and alert other troops. One component of the early warning system of the Ming Wall was the beacon towers. As an enemy approached, fires were lit in the towers. By day, smoke served to warn those down the Wall's line, and at night the fires lit up the darkened sky.

These towers paralleled the winding course of the Great Wall, but they were built not into the Wall itself but near the Wall on either side, depending on the lay of the land. A garrison was stationed at each tower, and the bases of these towers housed troops, contained storerooms, and even provided a stable for horses. Such beacon towers were built anywhere from a mile and a half to three miles apart. The use of beacon fires was not a Ming innovation, however; the practice was well established during the Qin and Han dynasties. The Ming simply perfected and extended the system and developed an elaborate signal code, issued by decree during the reign of Zheng Tong in 1446.

> The frontier troops are hereby ordered to set beacon fires. If one or two or up to 100 enemies are found, light one beacon fire and fire one salvo. If the enemy numbers 500, light two beacon fires and fire two salvos. Three beacon fires and three salvos indicate more than 1,000 enemy forces. Four fires and four salvos are for upwards of 5,000 troops. Five fires and five salvos correspond to more than 10,000 enemies.

Zheng Tong issued a royal order reminding those on border duty of the significance of the beacons and of what would happen to anyone who failed in his duty on the Wall:

> The beacon towers, together with their guards, must be inspected regularly. Stocks must be stored in quantity, and lookouts placed around the clock. In case of emergency, raise smoke in the daytime, or light a fire by night, to pass on the alert. See to it that no damage is done to the towers, so as to ensure prompt communication. Those who convey the information quickly and help defeat the enemy will be rewarded. Violators shall be punished according to military law.

Soldiers on the Great Wall kept themselves busy in times of both war and peace. When not manning the ramparts against enemy assault or signaling the next tower, the garrison soldiers served as inspectors for caravans of merchants passing by, maintained and repaired their section of the Wall, and even tended garden patches where they grew fresh vegetables for the garrison table.

This engraving shows the abundant structures dotting the Wall. Unfortunately, by the early seventeenth century, the Chinese empire—including the Great Wall—was in a state of decline. As soldiers deserted the garrisons, the Wall fell into disrepair.

Supplementary structures along the Wall included the *cheng* (fort), the *hou* (outpost), and the *zhang* (walled encampment). The *cheng* was built on the Chinese side of the wall to garrison additional troops sent to a given section to fight an encroaching enemy. The *zhang* was another variation on the garrison fort. It was a walled encampment, often built in the direct path of a possible enemy route. A primary difference between a *cheng* and a *zhang* was that a *zhang* housed no civilian personnel. The result of all these military installations was the greatest defensive line in Chinese history.

THE DECLINE OF THE MING DYNASTY

China enjoyed great prosperity as well as military security during Wanli's first decade as emperor, primarily through extensive trade with the West and expanding agriculture. Portuguese traders introduced European trade goods directly to China, including the latest cannon designs, which the emperor ordered installed at key Chinese fortifications, including several along the Great Wall.

In his last years as emperor, Wanli's hold over China weakened. He faced many problems, including the death of his most trusted and capable adviser, Zhang Zhu Zheng. Without Zhang, Wanli ruled in an increasingly erratic manner. He began to live extravagantly and fell prey to increased belief in superstitions, including a fear of "eclipses, comets, sudden floods or droughts." By 1599 his country stood on the brink of economic collapse. The emperor had spent millions of ounces of silver on his own family and those of court royalty, 9 million ounces on the building of royal palaces alone. One bureaucrat of the day described the situation grimly: "The treasuries of the provinces are empty. All enterprises are at a standstill. The Emperor withdraws himself from his people; for more than twenty years he has never called a council of his great ministers. The empire is in danger of revolution."

As Wanli increasingly confined himself within the walls of his elaborate palaces, he lost touch with his empire. The economy took a severe downturn with shortages in raw materials and food supplies. Not only the Great Wall but other construction projects completed during his reign, such as elaborate dike and canal systems, were abandoned, resulting in repeated flooding across the northern Chinese farmlands. Silverberg provides a clear picture of the beginning of the end of the Ming dynasty:

> The Great Wall, which had been so energetically rebuilt in the early years of Wanli's reign, now began to deteriorate again as the Emperor's life dragged on into the seventeenth century. The garrisons along the Wall were left without pay or supplies, and many soldiers deserted. By the time Wanli died in 1620, the empire was in a state of collapse, and within a further twenty-five years China would once again fall under "barbarian" rule—this time for nearly three centuries.

THE END OF THE GLORY DAYS

Wanli's death in 1620 marked the end of the Ming dynasty and the long, steady decline of the empire. Although three other Ming family members ruled China before control passed to other hands, Wanli's death left the Ming without a strong ruler. The Wall, which Wanli had ignored in his final years, did little to hold back the invading forces it was intended to block.

With the passing of the Ming dynasty, the glory days of the Great Wall of China came to an end. Already the Wall was decaying, abandoned to the northern tribes. The garrisons were abandoned and the bricks began to slip out of place, one by one, until the great Chinese dragon was rendered powerless to defend the noble culture that gave it life.

EPILOGUE

Much of the Great Wall of China lies in ruins today, the victim of centuries of harsh weather and neglect. Recent history has hastened the destruction of what one eighteenth-century Englishman described as "certainly the most stupendous work of human hands."

During the 1960s, China underwent a cultural revolution in which political, intellectual, and cultural traditions were—by government decree—deemed hateful. A twenty-year campaign of destruction followed, during which all things ancient were considered counterrevolutionary and regarded as rubbish. Historian Arthur Waldron explains:

> Beginning in 1966, priceless rare books were systematically burned, ancient bronzes melted for scrap, and people with learning tortured and killed. The Great Wall did not escape either. During the Cultural Revolution hundreds of kilometers were destroyed, sometimes with

At these and other fortifications, soldiers have guarded their country's borders for the greater part of Chinese history. Today, however, much of the Great Wall lies in ruins.

A WALL HOAX CAUSES REBELLION

One of the most bizarre stories connected with the Great Wall of China occurred nearly a century ago, with very serious results. The incident began in 1899 at a Denver railroad station, where four reporters representing the city's four newspapers—the *Post*, *Times*, *Republican*, and *Rocky Mountain News*—awaited the arrival of a train carrying an important visitor. When the visitor did not arrive that evening, the reporters found themselves without a story. Rather than return to face their editors, the reporters concocted a false report about a group of American engineers who were passing through Denver, bound for China at the behest of the emperor. Their purpose was to examine the Great Wall and to lay out plans for tearing it down. According to the fanciful news story, the Chinese government was ordering the dismantling of the Wall as a symbolic gesture to encourage further foreign trade. When the article hit the streets—with the headline "GREAT CHINESE WALL DOOMED!"—other papers picked up the story, including one in New York that added more details to the already baseless tale.

By the time the story reached China, the reaction was outrage. In the Chinese version, the American military was preparing to sail to China to tear down the Wall by force. China was already experiencing antiforeign sentiment and this perceived threat to the Wall was a spark that lit a powderkeg.

By the summer of 1900, rioting that became known as the Boxer Rebellion had broken out in China. Chinese rebels lay siege to many foreign embassies in Beijing. As violence increased, several European nations organized an invasion force that moved on Beijing to put down the threat to their embassies and to European citizens living in China.

In the end, the rebellion was smashed and order restored, but at the cost of the lives of thousands of Chinese. The rebellion proved just how important a symbol the Great Wall was to the people of China.

Members of the Red Guard march in Beijing during the Cultural Revolution, a twenty-year campaign of unprecedented destruction of all things ancient. During this dark chapter in Chinese history, huge portions of the Great Wall were destroyed.

dynamite and quarrying machinery, and the material used for road, reservoir, and building construction. Peasants took stone from the Wall to build houses for themselves and shelters for their livestock.

Sections of the Great Wall that had withstood the forces of millennia could not escape the modern-day scourge of a government determined to destroy all ties with the past.

The 1980s brought a reversal of China's disastrous campaign of destruction, however. In 1984, Chinese leader Deng Xiaoping signaled new life for his country's most visible historical monument when he publicly announced: "Let us love our country and restore our Great Wall." Almost immediately, the Chinese government began a campaign to rebuild large portions of the Great Wall. Today, hundreds of miles of the Wall are being restored, but much work remains to be done on the Great Wall if it is to be fully restored to its original condition.

For many Chinese, rebuilding the Great Wall has become an important act of patriotism.

Militarily obsolete, its importance is symbolic; today tourists visit the Wall near Beijing, where they can walk up and down a carefully restored and maintained section of this massive monument to the ancient past. The Great Wall has won a place of permanence in the minds of the people of China. It has become the symbol of their past, of their enduring civilization and

The Great Wall of China stands as a monument to China's enduring civilization.

of their own durability as a people of the modern age. In this Wall may lie the identity of the whole of China.

Perhaps the words of writer and Wall visitor Emile Hoveluque, who stood upon the ancient Wall's ramparts in 1919, best describe the state of the Great Wall as a continuing symbol of thousands of years of Chinese civilization:

> During fourteen centuries [China's walls] protected China and isolated her from the whole world: they are one of the forces which have made and preserved her civilization. They have fulfilled their task. They can crumble away. . . . Like a dead dragon, the wall undulates over the barren ridges. In its ruin and indescribable desolation it keeps its majesty. No human monument moves the human imagination more than this barrier on which the tides of barbarians have so often beaten, and which enabled this strange realm of China to gradually shape itself and to endure.

FOR FURTHER READING

Lai Po Kan, *The Ancient Chinese*. Morristown, NJ: Silver Burdett, 1981.

Robert Knox, *Ancient China*. New York: Warwick Press, 1979.

Peter Nancarrow, *Early China and the Wall*. Minneapolis: Lerner Publications, 1980.

Ronald Schiller, "China's Great Wall of Wonder," *Reader's Digest*, July 1982, pp. 67–73.

Lin Yutang, *The Chinese Way of Life*. Cleveland and New York: World Publishing, 1959.

WORKS CONSULTED

Paul H. Clyde and Burton F. Beers, *The Far East*. Englewood Cliffs, NJ: Prentice-Hall, 1971.

Jonathan Fryer, *The Great Wall of China*. London: New English Library, 1975.

William Edgar Geil, *The Great Wall of China*. London: John Murray, 1909.

Jacques Gernet, *A History of Chinese Civilization*. New York: Cambridge University Press, 1982.

Robin Hanbury-Tenison, *A Ride Along the Great Wall*. Topsfield, MA: Salem House, 1987.

Brian Hook, ed., *The Cambridge Encyclopedia of China*. New York: Cambridge University Press, 1982.

Peter Jenkins, *Across China*. New York: William Morrow, 1986.

Yu Jin, *The Great Wall*. Beijing: Cultural Relics Publishing House, 1980.

Michael Loewe, *Everyday Life in Early Imperial China*. London: Batsford, 1968.

Steve Mirsky, "The Great Green Wall," *Earth*, vol. 3, no. 6, November 1994, p. 11.

Frederick W. Mote and Denis Twitchett, eds., *The Cambridge History of China: The Ming Dynasty, 1368–1644*, vol. 7. New York: Cambridge University Press, 1988.

Rene Poirier, *Engineering Wonders of the World: The Stories Behind the Greatest Engineering Feats in History*. New York: Random House, 1993.

Robert Silverberg, *The Great Wall of China*. Philadelphia: Chilton Books, 1965.

————, *The Long Rampart: The Story of the Great Wall of China*. Philadelphia: Chilton Books, 1966.

Audrey Topping, "China's Incredible Find," *National Geographic*, vol. 153, no. 4, April 1978, pp. 440–59.

Denis Twitchett and Michael Loewe, *The Cambridge History of China: The Ch'in and Han Empires, 221 B.C.–A.D. 220*, vol 1. New York: Cambridge University Press, 1986.

Arthur Waldron, *The Great Wall of China: From History to Myth*. New York: Cambridge University Press, 1990.

Luo Zewen and Zhao Luo, *The Great Wall of China in History and Legend*. Beijing: Foreign Languages Press, 1986.

Luo Zewen et al., *The Great Wall*. London: Michael Joseph, 1981.

INDEX

PICTURE CREDITS

ABOUT THE AUTHOR

Tim McNeese received a bachelor's degree from Harding University in Searcy, Arkansas, and a master's degree in history from Southwest Missouri State University. He taught secondary-level history, English, and journalism for sixteen years, and is currently associate professor of history at York College.

He has written twenty books for young readers, including two eight-part series, *Americans on the Move* and *American Timeline*, and four books for the *Building History Series*. He coedited volumes I and II of the college texts *History in the Making: Sources and Essays of America's Past*.

Tim and his wife, Bev, live in York, Nebraska, with their daughter, Summer, and their son, Noah, who attends York College. They share their home with two Siamese cats and a cocker spaniel named Franklin. Tim enjoys woodworking, traveling, reading, and writing.